BLUE BOOK 60 is published in the United States by X60 MEDIA, LLC

© 2017 by X60 MEDIA, LLC

Created by Billy Martin and Tim Malloy

For Officials / Umpire resources visit: **ref60.com**

Necessary corrections and subsequent updates can be found at:

bluebook60.com

First Printing: June 2009
Second Printing: March 2010
Third Printing: March 2011
Fourth Printing: March 2012
Fifth Printing: March 2013
Sixth Printing: February 2014
Seventh Printing: February 2015
Eighth Printing: February 2016
Ninth Printing: January 2017

FORWARD

Welcome to the ninth release of *"Blue Book 60" – 2017 Fast Pitch Softball Edition*.
This printed reference book is a complimentary piece to our online educational community,
"60 Seconds on Officiating." This dynamic website features interviews, stories, rule
explanations, and officiating/coaching philosophy … all designed to be digested in
"about a minute." The "60 Second" concept started with basketball in 2008, expanded to
fast pitch softball in spring 2009, and is now updated yearly with the latest rule changes and
additions.

We encourage you to visit *bluebook60.com* for the latest updates to this guide and
ref60.com to join our community. 100 percent of the proceeds from this book are used for
continuing education of officials and coaches in 80+ countries worldwide.

We hope you enjoy reading *"Blue Book 60"* as much as we did creating it.

*"Your knowledge of the rules is something
that always can be questioned. So know them!"*

-Billy Martin, Co-Author
*Former Supervisor of Basketball Officials – IAABO Camden, NJ Board 34
NCAA Fast Pitch Umpire for Eastern Collegiate Softball Umpires
Scholastic Fast Pitch Umpire for the NJSIAA and West NJ Chapter #5*

"Rule competency breeds calmness and confidence in chaos."

-Tim Malloy, Co-Author
*Former College Basketball Official (CBOA) , Front Office Executive for Philadelphia 76ers,
Former Secretary/Independent Assignor and long standing member of
IAABO Camden, NJ Board 34*

ABOUT THE AUTHORS

Billy Martin has over 35 years officiating / umpiring experience with basketball and fast-pitch softball in the Southern New Jersey area.

Currently he is an NCAA umpire for the Eastern Collegiate Softball Umpires Association (ECSU) as well as a scholastic umpire for West (NJ) Chapter 5.

In the business world, Billy has more than 30 years of sales and marketing experience, and currently works with Salesforce (NYSE:CRM), the industry leader in Customer Relationship Management and marketing tools.

Billy holds a Master's Degree in Education (MEd) from The College of New Jersey specializing in Sports Medicine and a Master's Degree in Business Administration (MBA) from the University of Phoenix in Technology Management.

He is the co-author of the best-selling series of basketball officiating guides called, "Beyond the Rules" (**gobeyondtherules.com**) and co-founder of "60 Seconds on Officiating" the destination site for over 100,000 officials in 80 countries worldwide (**ref60.com**).

Billy resides in Wildwood, NJ and loves boating, fishing, and just about any activity that will leave sand between his toes.

Contact Billy Martin:
Email: billymartin@comcast.net
Twitter: @crmbilly or @ref60
LinkedIn: in/crmbilly

ABOUT THE AUTHORS

Tim **Malloy**, between the ebb and flow of a chronic illness that has required 32 surgeries, has pushed forward and carved a path of distinction in both the world of basketball and business.

As a 40+ year veteran referee of IAABO Board 34, Tim has worked numerous New Jersey state playoff games and climbed the ladder to the college ranks. Tim officiated as a member of CBOA where he earned Division II and III playoff assignments.

Off the court, Tim was a front office executive for the NBA World Champion Philadelphia 76ers in 1983 and served as the team's Assistant Group Sales Director and Public Relations Director for seven seasons. Tim later worked as a Sales and Promotions representative for Converse Inc., where he was a two-time Salesman-of-the Year award winner. He also holds a U.S. Patent for a golf training device that received a 4-star rating in Golf Magazine and is the co-author of the sports reference books, *Blue Book 60* for fast pitch softball and "*Beyond the Rules*" for basketball.

Tim is a graduate of St. Joseph's University (PA) and resides in West Deptford, NJ with his wife Pattie, son Matt and daughter Mary Frances.

Contact Tim Malloy via email:
board34@comcast.net

CONTRIBUTORS

We would like to give special thanks to all those who have given support and editorial contribution to make this project successful and have shared their knowledge with officials worldwide. Your expertise is greatly appreciated.

Allison J. Munch is the current New Jersey State Interscholastic Athletic Association's (NJSIAA) Rules Interpreter and former rules committee member of the NFHS. She also currently serves as the West Chapter #5 Cadet Supervisor. Allison has umpired all levels of softball including high school, NCAA Nationals, and the ASA Nationals for over 40 years. She has mentored hundreds of successful softball officials throughout New Jersey and the Delaware Valley.

Ed Sadowski was formerly the USSSA's Fast Pitch Umpire in Chief for the state of New Jersey. An NCAA Umpire with post-season and national championship experience, he also works at the scholastic level for the New Jersey State Interscholastic Athletic Association (NJSIAA) in its southern region.

Michael A. Schiro, Ph.D. came to officiating after a 15 year career as an NCAA Division II softball coach at Bloomfield College. He is currently Head Clinician and NCAA Rules Interpreter, for the Eastern Collegiate Softball Umpires (ECSU). Beginning his umpiring career in 1999, Mike has worked numerous ASA fast pitch tournaments at the state and regional level. In addition he has worked 8 fast pitch National tournaments including both the Men's and Women's Major and two 18 and under gold events. He is a member of the ASA Indicator Fraternity and has received the ASA Region 2 UIC Award for outstanding ability and loyalty. At the collegiate level, Mike has worked post season NCAA tournaments each year since 2006 umpiring at both the Division II and Division III levels. He has served as a regional UIC twice – once at the Division II level and once at Division III.

CONTRIBUTORS

Diane Reuter currently serves as President of the USSSA's South West New Jersey Umpires Association (SWNJUA) from inception. She has been involved with fast pitch softball in many capacities for over 25 years including umpiring for 15+ years for NFHS (West Chapter #5), USSSA, NSA, GSA, Pony and Little League. Diane has been honored to work multiple NJSIAA Southern New Jersey, Sectional and State finals as well as USSSA World Series Semi-Finals and Finals.

Don Briscoe is first and foremost a Board Member of the Duluth (Georgia) Softball Umpires Association. He is on the NCAA umpire staff of the Mid-Eastern Athletic Conference and seven other collegiate conferences, and currently serves as the Georgia State UIC for the United States Specialty Sports Association (USSSA). Don has umpired for 25+ years and has umpired 12 National/World Series tournaments for USA Softball, NSA, ISA and USSSA. Additionally Don has served as Umpire-in-Chief for two USSSA World Series.

Special thanks to the ...

Providing scholarships for individuals that desire to experience the joy of sports officiating.
Visit: ProjectZebra.org <u>or</u> www.project.zebra for more info.

REFERENCES

The **"BLUE BOOK 60"** series provides **OFFICIALS, UMPIRES, COACHES,** and **PLAYERS** a consolidated "**UNOFFICIAL**" reference guide that compares and contrasts the predominant rule governing bodies. Please refer directly to the official rule sets for each organization, as **"BLUE BOOK 60"** is intended to provide "60 second bites" of relevant content. **"BLUE BOOK 60"** is meant to complement the official publications, **NOT REPLACE** them.

(USSSA) United States Specialty Sports Association

The USSSA is a volunteer sport's governing body, non-profit organization based in Kissimmee, Florida. USSSA governs 13 sports across the US, Puerto Rico, various US Military bases, and Canada and has a membership of over 3.2 million.

USSSA Online News and Resources – www.usssa.com
611 Line Drive, Kissimmee, FL 34744 | Telephone: (321) 697-3636

(NFHS) National Federation of State High School Associations

The NFHS, from its offices in Indianapolis, Indiana, serves its 50 member state high school athletic/activity associations, plus the District of Columbia. The NFHS publishes playing rules in 16 sports for boys and girls reaching 18,500 high schools and over 11 million students involved in athletic and activity programs.

NFHS Publications Order Department – www.nfhs.org
P.O. Box 361246 | Indianapolis, IN 46236-5324 | Phone: (800) 776–3462

REFERENCES
(Continued)

USA Softball (Formerly ASA)

USA Softball (formerly ASA) is the National Governing Body (NGB) of Softball in the United States and a member of the United States Olympic Committee. Founded in 1933 as the Amateur Softball Association (ASA), USA Softball sanctions competition in every state through a network of 70 local associations and has grown from a few hundred teams in the early days to over 165,000 teams today, representing a membership of more than 2.02 million. USA Softball also annually registers over 25,000 umpires across the U.S.

Please Note

In an effort not to cause confusion with USSSA rules-- this BlueBook will reference USA Softball in various tables and charts as ASA – the former name of this national governing body.

USA Softball – www.usasoftball.com
2801 NE 50th Street |Oklahoma City, Oklahoma 73111 |Phone: (405) 424-5266

(NCAA) The National Collegiate Athletic Association

The National Collegiate Athletic Association (NCAA) is a voluntary organization through which many of the nation's colleges and universities govern their athletics programs.

NCAA Publications Online – www.ncaapublications.com
P.O. Box 6222
Indianapolis, Indiana 46206-6222
Phone: (317) 917-6222

ADDITIONAL RESOURCES

60 Seconds on Officiating:	**ref60.com**
Blue Book 60 Website:	**bluebook60.com**
Beyond the Rules (Basketball):	**gobeyondtherules.com**
Officiating Scholarships:	**projectzebra.org**

Logos and trademarks are property of their respective owners.
All rule references are copyrighted by their respective governing bodies.

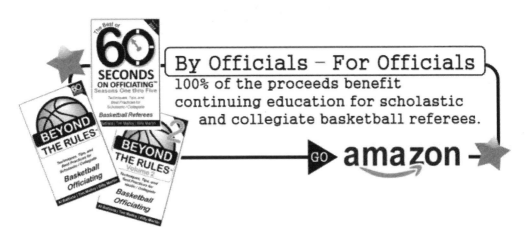

Visit

GoBeyondTheRules.com

for more information.

Also visit

Ref60.com

for articles and free basketball officiating resources.

2017 RULE CHANGES
NFHS (Scholastic)

2017 NFHS Major Rule Changes

1-5-2c: The taper is the transition area which connects the narrower handle to the wider barrel portion of the bat. The taper shall have a conical shape. Language requiring the taper to be of a solid surface has been removed.
Rationale: This change brings the NFHS in line with other rules codes concerning the surface of the taper.

3-2-1: While uniforms of team members shall be of the same color and style, state associations permit players to participate while wearing a different style uniform for various reasons, including inclement weather.
Rationale: There may be circumstances in which state associations make accommodations relative to inclement weather, religious exceptions, or other situations.

3-2-7: Exposed undergarments, if worn, are considered part of the official uniform. All exposed undergarments shall be a solid single color: black, white, gray or a school color.
> a. For individual players, exposed upper-body undergarments do not have to be the same color as exposed lower-body undergarments.
> b. For all team members, exposed upper-body undergarments shall be the same solid single color, and all exposed lower-body undergarments shall be the same solid single color.
> c. Garments other than team uniforms such as arm sleeves, leg sleeves, and tights are permissible. Anything worn on the arm or leg is a sleeve, except a brace, and shall meet the color restrictions.

Rationale: Multi-color undergarments and sleeves are a distraction and create a possible safety concern. This rule establishes solid color requirements similar to other NFHS sport rules.

3-2-15 NEW: All equipment shall be inspected by the umpire, and is to be placed outside the dugout/bench prior to the start of the game.
Rationale: Placing all equipment in one location at one time is a more efficient method to conduct this inspection.

3-6-7 PENALTY: Players and substitutes shall not enter the contest unreported. The umpire shall issue a team warning to the coach of the team involved and the next offender on that team shall be restricted to the dugout/bench for the remainder of the game. The head coach is also restricted to the dugout/bench for the remainder of the game for a second violation.

Rationale: Language clarifies when the coach is restricted to the dugout/bench.

2017 NFHS Points of Emphasis
1. Pitching
2. Uniforms
3. DP/FLEX Simplified

Reference: http://www.nfhs.org/
for complete rule changes and interpretations.

2017 RULE CHANGES
USA Softball (formerly ASA)

Please Note

In an effort not to cause confusion with USSSA rules-- this BlueBook will reference USA Softball in various tables and charts as ASA – the former name of this national governing body.

2017 USA Softball (ASA) Major Rule Changes

Rule 2 Section 3D The catcher's box shall be as wide as the two batter's boxes from outside line to outside line, 8'5" for Fast Pitch
Comment: Changes the depth of the catcher's box for all Fast Pitch Divisions of Play to seven feet.

Rule 4 Section 2 Rules shall be subject to requests for reasonable modification for purposes of complying with the Americans with Disabilities Act (ADA) unless such modifications would change the fundamental nature of the activity or would pose a significant risk to the safety of other participants.
Comment: Updates the ADA rule. See USA Softball rule references for more information.

Rule 4 Section 2B In appropriate circumstances, the following Rules may be used in the event a person is determined to be an ADA Player. In order for these ADA Flex Player, EP and DP rules to apply, the ADA player's specific disability shall correspond to the need for the application of these Flex Player, EP and DP rules.
Comment: Better defines what the ADA allows in the game of Softball.

Rule 4 Section 2J A participant who is hearing-impaired may use a sign language interpreter or other auxiliary hearing aid during play to assist that hearing-impaired participant. A sign language interpreter shall be allowed in the dugout, on the field of play (fair and foul territory), or in other areas in order to be able to provide communication to the hearing-impaired participant, but such sign language interpreter shall be subject to any other rules, policies or practices generally applicable to participants, including submitting to and passing an annual background check screening, if applicable.
Comment: Add wording to the ADA rule for the hearing-impaired.

Rule 5 Section 10 When time limit rule is in effect time it begins with the first warm up pitch.
Comment: Better defines when the time limit begins.

2017 USA Softball (ASA) Major Rule Changes (Continued)

Rule 5 Section 12D No person may knowingly possess or have under his/her control a weapon or explosive device on the playing field or in the dugout. For purposes of this subsection, a "weapon" means any firearm or any weapon of the kind usually known as slung shot, sand club, or metal knuckles, or any knife, dagger, dirk, or other similar weapon that is capable of causing death or bodily injury and is commonly used with the intent to cause death or bodily injury, but the definition of weapon shall specifically exclude an ordinary pocket knife or any softball-related equipment.
Comment: Adds wording to include weapons being banned from the dugout and playing field.

Rule 7 Section 1A Exception: Men's Fast Pitch, Men's Modified Pitch, Women's Fast Pitch and all Junior Olympic Fast Pitch Divisions of Play may use either on-deck circle as long as the on-deck batter is behind the batter and not on the batter's open side.
Comment: Adds the Women's Fast Pitch Classification of Play the ability to use either on-deck circle and clarifies the rule when the on-deck batter can use the opposite ondeck circle.

*Reference: http://www.usasoftball.com
for complete list of all rule changes.*

2017 RULE CHANGES
USSSA

Note: As of publication there are
NO Major Rule Changes in 2017 for USSSA

Source: USSSA Website Jan 1, 2017

2016 / 2017 RULE CHANGES
NCAA

2016 / 2017 NCAA Major Rule Changes

Rule 1.36 Obstruction Definition Changed
(Also 1.21, 9.4.1, 9.5.2.1, 9.5.2.4, 12.12.6.1, 12.15)
The act of a defensive team member that hinders or impedes a batter's attempt to make contact with a pitch or that impedes the progress of a runner who is legally running the bases, unless the fielder is in possession of the ball, is fielding a batted ball or is **in the act of catching a thrown ball**. The act may be intentional or unintentional and applies to live ball action only.

Rationale: Replaces "about to receive" with "in the act of catching" to better define the specific protected action. "About to receive" is to be considered a longer time frame than being "in the act of catching" a thrown ball.

Rule 2.1 Artificial Turf Guidelines Added
A synthetic turf surface field may be used for collegiate competition. It is recommended that the outfield portion be green and, if there is an infield portion, it be brown and have shorter blades than the outfield portion. Note: it is still highly recommended that a skinned infield be used (See Rule 2.14).

Rationale: Provides direction to those considering an artificial infield or outfield surface.

Rule 2.2 Backstop Padding Requirements
Regarding the backstop padding as noted in past rulebooks. When the backstop is wood, cement or brick, it **shall** be padded from dugout to dugout.

Rationale: Changes a recommendation (which was approved in 2011) to a requirement which goes into effect for the 2016 season.

2016 / 2017 NCAA Major Rule Changes (Continued)

Rule 2.17.2 Alternative / Non-Traditional Fields
(Also 12.12.3.7, 12.12.8.5)
When playing on a non-regulation field (i.e. a dome or multiuse facility) due to weather conditions, the field should have minimum fence distances as noted in Rule 2.11. If the actual fence distances are shorter and a fly, fair batted ball clears this distance, the batter shall be awarded a ground rule double, not a home run, and each base runner advanced two bases.

Rationale: Many makeshift facilities are too short to meet the minimum home run fence distances so in an effort to more closely reflect what would have happened had the field been regulation and to not skew player/team statistics, this clarifies that a ground rule double is awarded rather than an out–of-the-park home. Note this is to provide guidance for the alternative fields pressed into use due to weather conditions only.

Rule 2.22 (Old) Deletes the Runners Lane as a Required Line
(Also Table Diagrams ,12.2.8; 12.13.2; 12.19.1.3.2 and note 2; 12.25; App A)
Rationale: This change only changes the look of the field but has no effect on the batter-runner's responsibility to not interfere with the fielder receiving the throw at first base and she still cannot deviate from her basepath nor move backward if a fielder is attempting a tag play. However, because coaches do not teach the inefficiency of having their batter runners (especially slappers) hit the pitch, run to the lane, and then veer back to fair territory to touch first base, the runner's lane has become an unnecessary line on the field.

Rule 2.25 Stepping on Tarp (Effect)
If a fielder steps on the tarp, she will be considered to have entered dead-ball territory.

Rationale: There has been no effect listed for this rule violation previously.

Rule 3.3.1.1 Umpire's Use of Bat Rings
Deletes the umpire's use of a bat ring to determine if a bat is damages.

Rationale: Eliminates the unnecessary rule as umpires have not used bat rings for years as they inspect bats for damage.

Rule 3.3.1.8.5 Bat Barrel Color
Bat barrel shall be the color(s) "contrasting" to the ball.

Rationale: This change was first distributed to coaches and manufacturers prior to the start of the 2015 season as a request to not use bats with yellow barrels so that fielders would continue to be able to visually pick up the batted ball. At the time, there was no bat model routinely produced with an optic yellow barrel although custom bats could be ordered with any color barrel.

Rule 3.6.1 Pitcher's Glove
Deleted references that the pitcher's glove and its lacing shall be tan, brown, gray, white or black or any combination of those colors.

Rationale: Eliminates the restriction regarding the color of the pitcher's glove so they now are the same as fielder's gloves.

Rule 3.7.1 Helmet Finishes
All helmets shall be the same color and may not be a highly reflective, mirror-like chrome finish.

Rationale: The rules committee previously issued an interpretation that the highly reflective, mirror-like chrome finishes on helmets was not appropriate due to the distracting reflection of light. It is the committee's opinion that eliminating these gold, silver and bronze helmets minimizes injury risk to fielders.

Rule 3.10.2 Plastic Visors, Bandanas, and Hankerchiefs Now Permitted
Deletes that plastic visors, bandanas and handkerchiefs are not allowable headgear even if covered or worn under a cap or helmet.

Rationale: Eliminates the restriction on headgear which already allows caps and visors (by rule) as well as headbands of all kinds and bows (by not mentioning them). The rules committee feels they pose no physical risk and do not impact the image of the game negatively.

Rule 4.9 Spectator Interference (Effect)

If Spectator Interference clearly prevented a fielder from catching a fly ball in the field of play, the ball is dead, the batter is out, and the umpire shall award the appropriate compensation (for example, return base runners to bases, an out, or advance a runner) that, in his or her opinion, would have resulted had interference not taken place.

Rationale: Deletes wording about compensation for the offended team to allow the umpire to judge what is appropriate for both teams. For example without this change, if a spectator interfered with a fly ball that clearly would have been a sacrifice fly, the out would be declared but the runner not awarded home.

Rule 5.9.1 Streaming Video During Tournaments

Exception: A tournament host may stream video of all games in its tournament and are not restricted to filming and streaming video of only games in which it is a participant.

Rationale: Allows tournaments hosts to provide streaming of all the tournament games to enhance the experience by allowing family and friends to watch and to provide scouting opportunities for coaches.

Rule 5.11 Artificial Noisemakers

Defined: Objects used to make noise or amplify sound to show support, approval or opposition to playing action other than body parts are considered artificial noisemakers. The use of musical instruments or misuse of equipment to make noise are addressed separately in Rules 5.13 and 13.6.2 respectively.

Handling by Umpires: Changes "issue a warning to the offending individual" to "issue a team warning" in the effect and changes it from an administrative to behavioral ejection.

Rationale: These allow the umpire to warn a team one time rather than issue multiple warnings to specific individuals. In addition, it is more appropriately a behavioral rather than administrative issue.

Rule 6.19.1.9 Suspended Players Participating

Clarified if an ejected or suspended person is discovered to be participating again.

Rationale: Includes someone serving a suspension in the prohibition to participate further.

2016 / 2017 NCAA Major Rule Changes (Continued)

Rule 10.8 Illegal Pitch Not-Released (Effect Exception)
If an illegal pitch occurs but the pitch is not released, it is an immediate dead ball.

Rationale: Addresses the effect for a pitch never released.

Rule 10.10.5 Batter Hit by Pitch – Before Ball Reaches Plate Area
(Also 11.15.3.4)
Clarified: When the batter is hit by a pitch that has not yet reached the <u>front line of the batter's box</u>, assuming she did not swing or attempt to bunt.

Rationale: The old rule references a pitch not yet reaching home plate. This new change to reference "the front of the batter's box" is more appropriate with the number of slappers in the game who don't allow a pitch to get that deep. Effect: No pitch shall be declared. The ball is dead, and all subsequent action on that pitch is canceled.

Rule 10.14 Intentionally Pitching to Hit an Umpire (or Batter) Rules Separated
Regarding intentionally pitching at a batter or an umpire, separate the two actions so there can be different effects.

10.14.1 The pitcher shall not intentionally attempt to hit the batter with a pitch.

> *EFFECT (Unchanged)—If, in the umpire's judgment, such a violation has occurred, the umpire shall warn the pitcher, catcher and the head coach that future violations by any pitcher from his/her team will be cause for immediate ejection of the pitcher, catcher and the head coach. If, in the umpire's judgment, the situation warrants drastic action to diffuse a potentially volatile situation, the umpire may eject the pitcher and catcher without warning. The head coach of the offending team may also be ejected at this time if the umpire believes it is appropriate. A warning may be issued to one or both teams before the start of the game or at any time during a game if the umpire believes it to be appropriate (Behavioral ejections; see Rules 13.2.1 and 13.7). If the batter is hit by the pitch, the effect for hit by a pitch applies. (See Rule11.15)*

10.14.2 The pitcher shall not intentionally attempt to hit the umpire with a pitch.

> *EFFECT (New) —If, in the umpire's judgment, such a violation has occurred, the umpire shall eject the pitcher, catcher and the head coach (Behavioral ejections; see Rules 13.2.1 and 13.7). In addition, the head coach shall be suspended from the institution's next two previously scheduled and played contests in a traditional season (spring).*

2016 / 2017 NCAA Major Rule Changes (Continued)

Rationale: Leaves the effect as is for hitting the batter but separates out the effect for hitting an umpire so there is no warning just an immediate ejection of the pitcher, catcher and coach and suspension of the head coach.

Rule 11.21 Batter's Interference (Effect)
Delayed dead ball is signaled. The defensive team shall choose the result of the play or the batter is out and each base runner shall return to the base legally occupied at the time of the pitch.

Rationale: As with a violation for leaving a base early, the delayed dead ball gives the defense a chance to choose and keep the more advantageous play.

Rule 12.13.5 Runner Interfering (Taking-Out) a Fielder
The runner shall not slide out of the baseline nor slide outside her reach of the base she is attempting to slide into in order to slide directly at a fielder.

Rationale: Additional circumstances of unnecessary contact between players that result in the runner who targets the fielder rather than the base -- being called out and ejected (behavioral). Runners shall return to the base legally touched at the time of the infraction.

Rule 13.6.2 Misuse of Equipment (Effect)
When brought to the attention of the umpire by the opposing coach, the umpire shall issue a warning to the offending head coach. Subsequent violation shall result in the abused equipment being removed from the game (not returned to the dugout) and the ejection of the head coach (Behavioral Ejection).

Rationale: Holds the head coach accountable for the actions of his/her players after a warning is issued and removes the distraction for the umpire to identify the exact violator in the event of a subsequent violation (previously the violator is ejected).

Rule 13.8.4 Arguing Balls and Strikes Clarified / Expanded
Previously worded "arguing balls and strikes" is now changed to "question the strike zone and any call based purely on umpire's judgement."

EFFECT: A team warning shall be issued for the first offense in a game. Subsequent violations by the same team shall result in a behavioral ejection of the violator. All conditions for the effect of an in-game ejection apply. See Rule 13.2.

2016 / 2017 NCAA Major Rule Changes (Continued)

Note: A coach or player may, on occasion, request feedback regarding the specific location of a pitch or request a rule clarification without applying Rule 13.8.4 as long as it is not made in an argumentative manner and it does not delay play.

Rationale: "Questioning the strike zone" replaces "arguing balls and strikes" to allow for discussion of a called ball to be changed to a strike due to a checked swing. The constant questioning of judgement calls that will not be changed unnecessarily delays play and is often an unsporting act designed to ruin the opponent's momentum or stall for a player to warm-up. Either violation will now result in the perpetrator's ejection.

Rule 15.14.3 Filing of Incident Reports

In all cases involving an ejection of an NCAA player or team representative, the ejecting umpire is responsible for submitting an incident report.

Rationale: Eliminates the requirement for filing NCAA incident reports for violations by NAIA, USCCA, NJCAA and Cal JC offenders.

For more information and a complete list of rule changes download the NCAA Rulebook:
http://www.ncaapublications.com/p-4402-2016-and-2017-ncaa-womens-softball-rules.aspx

APPEALS – ALL TYPES

When an umpire does **NOT** make a ruling until **REQUESTED** by a **COACH** or **PLAYER** ...

This is considered an **APPEAL** play.

The various **TYPES** of appeals include:

- **DEAD BALL ONLY (VERBAL)**
  - Used for **BATTING OUT** of **ORDER** appeals.

- **LIVE (IMPLIED)** or **DEAD BALL (VERBAL)**
  - **MISSING** a **BASE** while advancing or returning.
  - **LEAVING** a base on a **CAUGHT FLY-BALL** before it is **TOUCHED.**

- **LIVE BALL ONLY (IMPLIED)**
  - **ATTEMPTING** to **ADVANCE** after making the turn at 1st base (overrunning the base).

Asking for help on a particular ruling is <u>NOT</u> considered an appeal, whether originating from another umpire or coach/player.

Rules Reference
USSSA 9.1 / NFHS 2-1 / ASA RS #1; 7-2d; 8-7i; 8-3g / NCAA 7.1.1

APPEALS – HOW THEY ARE MADE

Live ball appeals can be either **VERBAL** <u>or</u> **IMPLIED**.
Once the ball is dead **VERBAL** appeals are only allowed.

LIVE (VERBAL or IMPLIED):
- **IMPLIED**: Appeal by any fielder with the ball touching a base (left too soon/missed.)
- **IMPLIED**: By touching a runner that violated –before returning even if standing on another base.
- If in the pitching position, pitchers should step backward to avoid an illegal pitch.

DEAD (VERBAL ONLY):
- Once runners complete advancement and time is granted by the umpire it becomes a dead ball appeal.
- Manager, coach or any defensive player can make a verbal appeal on specific player.
- If the ball was thrown out of play – runners are permitted to complete their base running responsibilities before the umpire may rule on any requested appeal.
- **NFHS**: Pitcher can make verbal appeal while contacting the pitching plate with no illegal pitch penalty.
- **ASA**: Infielders may appeal only.
- **USSSA, NFHS, and NCAA**: a coach or any fielder may make an appeal.

Even though more than one appeal can be made (on a base or player) it should not become a guessing game for coaches or players.

Rules Reference
USSSA 9.1 / NFHS 2-1 / ASA RS #1/ NCAA 7.1.1

APPEALS – MISCELLANEOUS

Appeals **MUST BE** made **PRIOR** to the next legal or illegal pitch, or at the end of an inning before all infielders (including the pitcher) leave fair territory (and the catcher vacates position), or on the last play of the game before the umpires leave the field of play.

- **RUNNERS** may **ADVANCE** during a **LIVE** BALL appeal once pitcher no longer has possession of the ball in the circle (or makes play on runner).

- **LIVE BALL** appeals can even be made after a play is attempted on a runner.

- Once **TIME** is called by the umpire, no runner may advance.

- Runners may **NOT RETURN** to touch a missed base once:
  - They reach a base beyond the base missed or left too soon on a dead ball appeal.
  - They leave the field of play.
  - A following runner has scored.

- **MORE** than **ONE** appeal may be made on a play, but should not be a guessing game.

- Missing **HOME PLATE** (along with a missed or no-tag) can be appealed by tagging runner (or plate) with the ball.

- If the appeal was a **FORCED 3rd OUT**, then prior runs would **NOT** score.

Tag-ups are considered "time plays" and not "force outs," therefore any appeal on leaving a base too soon might result in the scoring of a run prior to the 3rd out.

Rules Reference
USSSA 9.1; 9.3 / NFHS 2-1 / ASA RS #1/ NCAA 7.1.1

BALL LODGES ᴵɴ UNIFORM

NFHS / ASA / NCAA:

A ball that becomes accidently lodged in a
<u>defensive</u> player's uniform shall **REMAIN LIVE** until the umpire
judges the ball is no longer playable.

- Other codes do not specifically reference this unique situation.
- **NCAA**: If the ball becomes lodged in an offensive player's uniform the ball becomes dead immediately.
- However, if a batted ball becomes lodged in a defensive player's uniform, this should **NOT** be considered a legal **CATCH**.

 *Although not specifically addressed by rule, deliberately hiding a live ball inside a uniform to deceive base runners may be considered unsportsmanlike conduct and penalized based on the situation.*

Rules Reference
USSSA-NR / NFHS 5-1 / ASA 8-4g / NCAA 9.8.2; 9.8.3

BALL ROTATION PROCEDURE

The current **GAME BALL** is typically in play until such time as it goes out of play, blocked, or the umpire deems the ball unsuitable for play from damage.

SITUATION	USSSA	NFHS	ASA	NCAA
If BOTH Balls Do NOT Get Into Play After 1st Half Inning	*Must Throw Unused Ball to Start Bottom Half of Inning*			*No Reference*
Pitcher Has a Choice of Balls to Start Subsequent Innings	√	√	√	*Choice for Any Inning*
Compare TWO Balls Side-by-Side when Choosing	*Not Permitted - Must Use Other Ball Given to Pitcher by Umpire*			*Must return ball before receiving another.*
Pitcher MAY Request a New Ball			*OK to Remove if UnPlayable*	*At Any Time*
Strict Ball Rotation Procedures During Inclement Weather Conditions	*May Not Apply Based on Umpire Discretion*			*None*

NCAA Note: *For all NCAA games 12 balls are required to be available (2 New + 10 Good) Pitchers also may request a new ball at any time during the game.*

Rules Reference
USSSA 2007 Clarifications pg. 4 / NFHS Umpire Manual
ASA RS #2 / NCAA 10.12

BAT – LEGAL / ILLEGAL

SPECIFICATIONS	USSSA	NFHS	ASA	NCAA
General Requirements	All bats must be smooth, straight, un-altered, have a closed barrel end and pass through a 2 ¼ " diameter ring.			
Knobs	Securely Fastened by Mechanical Attachment or Welded			
Grip Length	10" min- 15" max		6" min- 15" max	10" min - 15" max
Required Certification Mark on Bat	USSSA BPF 1.20 or Less // New USSSA Mark on Taper in 2014	ASA Approved 2000, 2004, or 2013 Mark.		Visible ASA Approved 2004 Seal
Wood Bats	Legal in all codes (Except NCAA)			
Bat List	Not Applicable	Bat Must Not Appear on ASA Banned Bat List		Coach must provide NCAA Bat List for each game
Maximum Length	34 " Maximum Length			
Maximum Weight	38 oz. Maximum Weight			
Material Types	All Codes Permit Use of Wooden Bats - along with Metal, Fiberglass, Graphite, or Composite.*			
One Piece Rubber Grip and Knob	Illegal			Flare / Cone Shape is Illegal
Tacky Substance End Point	15" from End of Handle			On Grip Only
Slightly Dented Bats	No Flat Spots or Dents	No Burrs or Dents Permitted even if ring fits over.		No Burrs or Dents
Warming Devices	Approved Models Permitted	Illegal: Bats Found in Device are Altered	Not Approved	Prohibited - Renders Bat Altered

Additionally:

USSSA stipulates the bat shall not have choke up devices, exposed rivets, pins, rough or sharp edges or any form of exterior fastener that would present a hazard. Bats shall be free of rattles and burrs.

NFHS allows the bat taper to be rough but it must be solid. No choke up devices are permitted.

NCAA: Wooden Bats are NOT permitted for batting use in NCAA games but may be used in the on-deck warm-up circle.

BAT – LEGAL / ILLEGAL
(Continued)

 **ALTERED BATS** shall include any legal bat that is tampered with by removing or replacing parts, painting, thinning walls, lathing, rolling, heating, cooling, or changing the performance characteristics from the original manufacturer.

Use of Altered (or Non-Approved Bat)				
	USSSA	**NFHS**	**ASA**	**NCAA**
Effect on Batter (If Enters Box)	Called Out if Hits Ball with Bat Before Next Pitch*	Completes at Bat -- Batter is Out - Ejected and Coach Ejected	Ejected from Game / Tourney	Out and Ejected
Effect on Runners	Runners Return to the Position Occupied BEFORE the Illegal Bat was Used			
Prior Play / Outs	Any Outs Occuring PRIOR to the Discovery of the Illegal Bat will Stand			
Warning Issued	None			
Player Removal	Suspension if Bat is Sent for Testing Pending Results	Ejected	Ejected from Game / Tourney	Ejected
Coach Removal		Ejected		Ejected**

The use of an **ILLEGAL**, **ALTERED**, or **BAT** that has been **REMOVED** from the game previously, carries various penalties from the batter being declared out to both player and coach removal from the game.

*USSSA Note: There is no violation until the batter "hits" the ball with the illegal bat fair/foul. She may change bat if detected while in the batter's box. The batter is out only if she hits the ball and it's discovered before the next pitch, legal or illegal. There is no penalty if a base on balls.

**NCAA Note: The head coach is ejected only when a bat that umpires have declared inappropriate and has been removed from the team's set of allowable bats and is then brought to the plate by the batter.

ASA Effect: Batter is out, all outs count and all runners return to the base occupied at the time of the pitch.

 *USSSA tournament directors have defined procedures to address potential illegal or altered bats when suspected in tournament play. These include inspection and potential removal of the bat for further testing.*

Rules Reference
USSSA 2.10.A-D; 8.18.x; 7.14.A; 3.5 / NFHS 1-5; 3-6-1; 7-4-2
ASA 7-4b to i; 7-6B / NCAA 3.3

BATTER HITS BALL TWICE

BATTER HITS BALL a SECOND TIME

Batter is Still __IN__ Box	USSSA	NFHS	ASA	NCAA
Bat Hits Ball a Second Time	Dead Ball - Foul Ball			
Batted Ball Hits Batter	Dead Ball - Foul Ball			

Batter is __OUT__ of Box*	USSSA	NFHS	ASA	NCAA
Batted Ball Hits Batter's Body in __FAIR__ Territory	Dead Ball - Batter is Declared Out			
Batted Ball Hits Bat While Still in Batter's Hands in __FAIR__ Territory	Dead Ball - Batter is Declared Out			
Batted Ball Hits Batter's Body in __FOUL__ Territory	Dead Ball - Foul Ball			
Batted Ball Hits the Bat While Still in Batter's Hands in __FOUL__ Territory	Dead Ball - Foul Ball			
A Dropped Bat Hits a Batted Ball in __FAIR__ Territory	Dead Ball - Batter is Declared Out			
A Batted Ball __ROLLS__ into a Dropped Bat in __FAIR__ Territory	Ball is __LIVE__ and In Play -- Unless the Batter Intentionally Tried to Interfere with the Ball			

*Batter is __OUT__ of Box means: Batter first legally contacted the ball while IN the batter's box and then was contacted by the ball a second time, OUT of the batter's box.

Rules Reference

USSSA 7.14.F / NFHS 7-4-13 Exception / ASA 7-6K; RS #24 / NCAA 11.14

BATTER PREVENTS BALL FROM ENTERING STRIKE ZONE

If the batter **PREVENTS** the ball from **ENTERING** the strike zone by any method **OTHER** than hitting the ball <u>**OR**</u> a pitched ball **HITS** a **BATTER** while the **BALL** is **IN** the strike zone:

- ⚾ The play is considered a **DEAD-BALL** strike.

- ⚾ The **BALL** is **DEAD**.

- ⚾ A **STRIKE** is given to the batter.

- ⚾ **RUNNERS** must **RETURN** to original bases occupied at the time of pitch.

NCAA Only: When the batter is hit by a pitch that has **not yet reached the front line** of the batter's box, assuming she did not swing or attempt to bunt.

- ⚾ The **BALL** is **DEAD.**

- ⚾ It is declared a **NO-PITCH.**

NFHS: Intentionally preventing the ball from entering the strike zone and making a travesty of the game can result in either a warning for unsportsmanlike conduct, restriction to the bench, or even ejection based on the umpires judgment.

<u>*Rules Reference*</u>
USSSA 7.5B / NFHS 7-2-1h / ASA 7-4L / NCAA 10.10.5, 11.15.3.4

BATTER STEPS OUT OF THE BOX

ACTION				
	USSSA	NFHS	ASA	NCAA
Batter Must Occupy Batter's Box	*Within 10 Seconds After Umpire Directs Batter to Take Box or Pitcher is Ready to Pitch*			
Failure to Occupy Batter's Box within Time Limit	*Ball is Dead - Strike is Given to Batter - Batter is Called Out if 3rd Strike*			
Batter Permitted to Step Out of Box Between Pitches (No Time Requested)	*Permitted but Risks Being Charged with Delay*		*Must Keep At Least ONE Foot in the Box While Taking Signals*	*Permitted but Risks Delay*
Batter Requests Time	*Umpire's Discretion to Grant Time Out - May Deny Request Based on Situation*			

*Individual rule sets vary, but generally, if a batter **REQUESTS** time-out and it is **NOT GRANTED** but steps out of the box **ANYWAY**:*

- If the pitcher **DELIVERS** the ball to the plate, the live ball may be called a **STRIKE** on the batter, regardless of pitch location (USSSA / NFHS) or may be called a **BALL** or **STRIKE** (based on location) for ASA / NCAA.
- If the pitcher **DELAYS** delivering the ball, the umpire shall declare a "no pitch" and the batter shall be directed to return to the batter's box and play ball or risk violating the time rule <u>and</u> the pitcher shall be directed to pitch the ball.

The **BATTER** shall not deliberately try to **DRAW** an illegal pitch. This act can result in a warning, restriction or ejection. The **UMPIRE** may elect to **GRANT** time-out based on the situation.

Rules Reference
USSSA 7.8 / NFHS 7-3-1 / ASA 7-3B&C / NCAA 11.2

BATTER POSITIONING

The batter is required to **TAKE** a **POSITION** within either of the two batters boxes when directed by the umpire.

ACTION / EFFECT	USSSA	NFHS	ASA	NCAA
Batter Switches Batter's Boxes when Pitcher is in Position and Ready to Pitch	*All Codes (Except NCAA*): Ball is Dead and Batter is Out for Disconcerting the Pitcher – Runners Must Return.* *NCAA: Delay Dead Ball and the Defensive team shall choose either the result of the play or batter is out and each runner return.*			
Batter Hits a Fair or Foul Ball While Either Foot is Touching Completely Outside of Batter's Box	*Dead Ball - Batter is Out*			
Batter Hits a Fair or Foul Ball While Either Foot is Touching Home Plate	*Dead Ball - Batter is Out*			
Batter Intentionally Erases a Chalk Line (First Offense)	*No Reference*	*Strike Given to Batter*	*No Reference*	*Strike Given to Batter*
Batter Intentionally Erases a Chalk Line (Second Offense)	*No Reference*	*Both Offender and Coach Restricted to Bench*	*No Reference*	*Strike Given to Batter*

*(See section – **Erasing Chalk Lines**)*

Rules Reference
USSSA 7.4b; 7.8 / NFHS 3-6-17; 7-4-3; 7-4-8 / ASA 7-3d; RS-#7
NCAA 2.15.4, 11.21, 11.15, 11.21.1, 11.22

BATTER STRUCK BY PITCH

If a pitch **NOT SWUNG** at **STRIKES** the **BATTER,** they are awarded first base without liability to be put out, provided:

A batter is **HIT** by the **PITCH** which is in the **STRIKE ZONE** or if a batter is **SWINGING** at the ball and is **HIT** by the **PITCH** is shall be considered a **DEAD BALL / STRIKE**.

No base is awarded – just a strike on the batter.

It does not matter if a pitched ball hits the **GROUND** before striking the batter – she is still awarded first base.

The struck batter is awarded first base even if the ball strikes the **UNIFORM** or **CLOTHING**, and not her body directly – **USSSA**: unless clothing is loose or unbuttoned.

- Runners advance only if **FORCED**.

- If the batter **OBVIOUSLY TRIES** to be struck by the pitch, the umpire will call either a **DEAD BALL / BALL** or **DEAD BALL / STRIKE** based on the location of the ball within the strike zone. Specifically **USSSA and NFHS** stipulates that no attempt to avoid being hit by the pitch is required. However, the batter may not obviously try to get hit by the pitch. **NCAA** stipulates the pitch must be entirely within and has reached the front line of the batter's box.

- The batter's **HANDS** are **NOT** considered to be part of the **BAT**.

- If the pitch is **WITHIN** the **BATTER's BOX**, the batter is **NOT REQUIRED** to **AVOID** being hit by the pitch.

Rules Reference
USSSA 8.4; 8.4d-note; 10.1; 10.3a / NFHS 7-3-2, 7-2-1g; 8-1-4b
ASA 7-4h to j; 8-1F / NCAA POE pg 5; 11.15

BATTER-RUNNER OVERRUNS FIRST

A batter-runner may **OVERRUN** first base and return directly to it without liability to be put out.

If she attempts to **ADVANCE** toward second base and decides to **RETURN** (to first) she is at risk to be tagged out.

However once the **PITCHER** has control of the live ball **WITHIN THE PITCHING CIRCLE** the following items may also apply:

The **BATTER-RUNNER** may **ROUND** first base (towards 2nd base), **STOP** momentarily, and then immediately **WITHOUT STOPPING** again …
- **RETURN** to first base.
- **OR** she may **ADVANCE** to second base.

Provided the **BATTER-RUNNER** stops **ONCE** momentarily then either **ADVANCES** or **RETURNS**, it shall be legal … but is at liability to be tagged out if the pitcher makes a play on her.

This includes a **BATTER-RUNNER** advancing from a walk, dropped 3rd strike, or any legal method while the ball is live.

NCAA Differences: After over-running first base and a batter-runner starts moving toward first base and before she touches that base she can go to either first base or second base – provided she stays within the extended base path. Once she makes a move toward **EITHER** base (steps outside the extended base path) she is committed to that base – either first or second, depending on which way she moved.

*(See **Look-Back Restrictions** section for more information)*
Rules Reference
USSSA 8.2; 8.10 / NFHS 8-7-2; 8-6-8; 8-7-4 / ASA 8-7T(3); RS #37 / NCAA 12.21.6.5

BATTER-RUNNER STEPS BACKWARD

For **ALL CODES:**

The ball becomes **DEAD IMMEDIATELY** if a batter-runner steps **BACKWARD** toward home plate to **AVOID** (or delay) being **TAGGED**.

⚾ The batter-runner is declared **OUT**.

⚾ **USSA-NFHS-ASA:** Other **BASE RUNNERS** must **RETURN** to the last base legally touched at the <u>time of the infraction</u> or **NCAA**, <u>time of pitch</u>.

Regarding USSSA, NFHS and ASA base runners, their location should be noted at the "time of infraction" and not the "time of pitch." If the base runner had legally occupied the next base before the infraction occurred, they should be permitted to stay (or return) to that base. Therefore, if the illegal action of the batter-runner is slow to develop, other base runners may have advanced legally before the infraction occurred. NCAA rules require runners to return to the last base legally touched at the "time of pitch", which can result in a different effect.

Rules Reference
USSSA 8.17G / NFHS 5-1-1n, 8-2-8 / ASA 8-2h; RS #33i / NCAA 12.2.10

BATTING - OUT OF ORDER

A **PROPER** batter is a player (or substitute) that follows the **PRECEDING** batter in the lineup. An **IMPROPER** batter is considered to be at bat when she **ENTERS** the batter's box and **ONE** pitch is thrown.

If an **IMPROPER** batter is discovered (while at bat), time may be requested, and the batter replaced by the **PROPER** batter, assuming the **IMPROPER** batter's ball/strike count – as long as this has been discovered **BEFORE** the **IMPROPER** batter has been put-out or becomes a base runner.

Only the **DEFENSIVE** team can **APPEAL** batting out of order, once the batter has completed her time at bat.

Batting out of order is an **APPEAL** play. **ONCE** the batter completes her at bat:

- It must be **APPEALED** prior to the next **LEGAL** (or **ILLEGAL**) pitch.
- The **BATTER** who **FAILED** to bat in her **PROPER** turn is declared **OUT**.
- Do **NOT** declare the **IMPROPER BATTER** out. Her time at bat is simply **NEGATED** and she is returned to the **BENCH**.
- **All Codes (Except NCAA):** All **OUTS STAND** and **RUNNERS** must return to their locations at the "time of pitch." In **NCAA**, all **OUTS** are **NULLIFIED**.
- Runners **ADVANCING** by stolen base, wild pitch, passed ball, or illegal pitch are **LEGAL**.

(Continued on Next Page)

BATTING - OUT OF ORDER
(Continued)

- Once an **IMPROPER BATTER** reaches base (or is put out) and a next (legal / illegal) **PITCH** is delivered – she is **NOW** considered the **PROPER BATTER**.
- Once the defensive team **LEAVES** the **FIELD** after the end of an inning, the **IMPROPER BATTER** is now considered to be the **PROPER BATTER**.
- Once an **IMPROPER BATTER** becomes the **PROPER BATTER**, her actions become legal and stands completely.

Once a **PROPER BATTER** is called **OUT** because she **FAILED** to bat in turn – the **NEXT** batter shall be the person whose **NAME FOLLOWS** the batter that was called out. <u>**For NCAA**</u>, this is true unless she is **ON BASE** ... in which case she is skipped and the **NEXT** batter is the proper batter.

Once an **IMPROPER BATTER's** actions are legalized, the **NEXT BATTER** shall be the person whose **NAME FOLLOWS** the legalized improper batter.

If **SEVERAL PLAYERS** bat out of order, and it's discovered when a **LEGALIZED** improper batter is on base while it's her turn to bat, she **REMAINS** on base and is **NOT** out.

NO RUNS may score on the play if properly appealed.

 *NCAA specifically states: The public-address announcer shall announce the players as listed on the lineup card. The public-address announcer, umpires or official scorer shall not call attention to the improper batter. If this occurs, the plate umpire shall warn the public-address announcer and/or the official scorer that on the next infraction, he/she will be removed from that position.*

<u>*Rules Reference*</u>
USSSA 9.10 / NFHS 7-1-2 / ASA 7-2a to f
NCAA 11.10 and Appendix B

BLOCKED BALL –DEFINED

A **BLOCKED BALL** results when a **LIVE** **BATTED,** **PITCHED,** or **THROWN** ball **CONTACTS** loose equipment or miscellaneous items (not being used legally in the game) in **LIVE** ball territory – or when a **LIVE** ball is **TOUCHED,** stopped, crosses into **DEAD BALL TERRITORY,** or is handled by a **PERSON** not engaged in the game.

This **EXCLUDES** – (**NOT** a **BLOCKED BALL**):
- Batters' **BAT** dropped legally.
- Catchers' **MASK** removed during play.
- **UMPIRES'** Equipment.
- Players' **HELMET** (**ACCIDENTLY** fallen).

This **INCLUDES** - (**LIVE BALL TOUCHING**):

- Or **HANDLING** by a **PERSON** not engaged in the game.
- Detached part of a player's **UNIFORM,** intentionally removed.
- **BATS / HELMETS / GLOVES** not properly removed from live ball area and placed in dugout appropriately.
- **PLAYERS' HELMET** that is **REMOVED INTENTIONALLY** while the ball is **LIVE** and left on the field - *(see **Helmet Requirements** for additional penalties).*
- **WARM-UP EQUIPMENT** not in possession of the **ON-DECK** batter.
- A thrown ball leaves the playing field and lands in **DEAD BALL TERRITORY.**

Rules Reference
USSSA 3.10 / NFHS 2-2-3; 5-5-1g; 8-6-15 / ASA 8-5g (3); RS-#17 / NCAA 9.8 – 9.14

BLOCKED BALL –EFFECT

TEAM at **BAT** causes a **BLOCKED <u>THROWN</u>** ball:
- ⚾ Immediate **DEAD BALL** (Interference)
- ⚾ **NFHS/ASA:** Runner being **PLAYED ON** is **OUT** with other runners **RETURNING** to last base touched prior to blocked ball. If **NO PLAY** is apparent then **NO RUNNERS** are **OUT** but runners **RETURN**, per above.
- ⚾ **USSSA / NCAA:** Runner **CLOSEST** to **HOME** is **OUT**. If **NO PLAY** is apparent then **NO RUNNERS** are **OUT** but runners **RETURN**.

DEFENSE causes a **BLOCKED <u>THROWN</u>** ball:
- ⚾ Immediate **DEAD BALL** (Interference)
- ⚾ **OVERTHROWN** ball rules apply – **RUNNERS** awarded **TWO-BASES** from the **RELEASE** of throw.

A **<u>FOUL BATTED</u> BALL:**
- ⚾ Touching loose equipment (**BLOCKED**) is a **FOUL BALL**.

TEAM at **BAT** blocks a **<u>FAIR BATTED</u> BALL:**
- ⚾ **DEAD BALL** – **RUNNERS ADVANCE** only if forced. (if **BATTER-RUNNER**) is awarded first base on a **HIT**.
- ⚾ If defense was **PREVENTED** from making play – same as **THROWN** ball (above).

DEFENSE blocks a **<u>FAIR BATTED</u> BALL:**
- ⚾ Immediate **DEAD BALL** (Interference)
- ⚾ **BATTER** and **RUNNER(S)** is **AWARDED TWO-BASES** from the **TIME** of **PITCH**.

Rules Reference
USSSA 8.18f; 10.3g / NFHS 2-2-3; 5-5-1g; 8-6-15 / ASA RS-#17 / NCAA 9.8-9.14

BUNT ATTEMPT

ACTION	USSSA	NFHS	ASA	NCAA
Hands / Wrists During the <u>BUNT</u> Attempt	*Non-Swinging Movement with Bat - <u>WRISTS are LOCKED</u> as Batter Attempts to Tap the Ball into Play*			
Hands / Wrists During the <u>SLAP HIT</u> Attempt	*Swinging Movement of the Bat - <u>WRISTS BREAK</u> During the Swinging Motion as Batter Attempts to Strike the Ball*			
Holding (Not-Withdrawing) the Bat within the Strike Zone During a Bunt Attempt	*Automatic Strike on the Batter UNLESS Bat is Moving AWAY from the Ball*		*If Bat is Not Moved Toward Ball can be a Ball or Strike Based on the Pitch*	*Same as USSSA and NFHS*
Bunt Attempt After Two Strikes	*If Foul Ball ... the Batter is Declared Out*			
Slap Hit Attempt After Two Strikes	*If Foul Ball ... the Batter Continues with Current Count*			

 *Attempting to legally **TAP** a ball while using any **NON-SWINGING** movement of the bat should be considered a **BUNT ATTEMPT**. Umpires should focus on the rolling of wrists, bat position / movement, and ball location relative to the strike zone.*

Rules Reference
USSSA 3.12 / NFHS 2-8-1; 2-8-2; 2-9-2 / ASA 7-6g & h; RS-#10 / NCAA 1.12

CATCH – DEFINED

When a fielder **SECURELY GAINS POSSESSION** of a batted, pitched, or thrown ball – using her hand(s) and /or glove-mitt, this is ruled a **LEGAL CATCH**.

First, the fielder must **CONTROL** the ball while the release of the ball must be **VOLUNTARY** and **INTENTIONAL**. It's considered a **LEGAL CATCH** if the ball is **DROPPED** while being **TRANSFERRED** to the throwing hand.

Fielders must have possession **BEFORE** going into (or touching) **DEAD BALL** area. If the fielder catches the ball **THEN FALLS** over (or through) a fence is still considered to have made a **LEGAL CATCH**.

A fielder may contact (or step on) a **COLLAPSIBLE FENCE** and still make a catch – provided it is not lying flat.

(See Section on **Collapsible Fences** for more details on legal catch vs. no catch situations)

These are **NOT** considered **LEGAL CATCHES**:

- ○ Catching with anything other than one's hands or glove in its **PROPER PLACE**.
- ○ **FALLING** to the ground and **NOT** maintaining **POSSESSION**.
- ○ Player uses glove (or uniform) which is **DISPLACED** from its proper position.
- ○ The defensive player's **ENTIRE FOOT** is touching **DEAD BALL** territory.
- ○ Once a fly ball **TOUCHES** anything other than a defensive player (while in flight) it will be considered a **GROUND** ball.
- ○ **TRAPPING** the ball against the ground before being caught.

Rules Reference
USSSA 3.14 / NFHS 2-9 / ASA 1C; 8-5k / NCAA 1.13, 9.1

CATCH and CARRY

A fielder that **UNINTENTIONALLY** carries a live ball from **PLAYABLE** territory into **DEAD BALL** territory:

- 🎾 Causes the ball to become **DEAD IMMEDIATELY**.

- 🎾 Each base **RUNNER** is awarded **ONE BASE** from the **LAST BASE TOUCHED** at the **TIME** of the **INFRACTION**.

If in the judgment of the umpire, a fielder **INTENTIONALLY** carries a live ball from **PLAYABLE** territory into **DEAD BALL** territory:

- 🎾 The ball becomes **DEAD IMMEDIATELY**.

- 🎾 Each base **RUNNER** is awarded **TWO BASES** from the **LAST BASE TOUCHED** at the **TIME** of the **INFRACTION**.

*The **TWO BASE** award also applies to a player **INTENTIONALLY** pushing, kicking, or throwing a live ball into dead ball territory. The runner's position should also be noted at the time when the infraction occurred.*

Rules Reference
USSSA 10.3i; 8.14c(5); 8.14.d(6) / NFHS 8-4-3 / ASA 1C; 8-5j & k / NCAA 9.3, 9.13

CATCHER RETURNS BALL TO PITCHER

In all codes, the catcher is required by rule to return the ball **DIRECTLY** to the **PITCHER** after each pitch.

These are some **EXCEPTIONS** where the catcher **MAY** throw the ball to another player, other than the pitcher:

🥎   After a **STRIKE OUT** is made.

🥎   After an actual or attempted **PUT-OUT** is made by the catcher.

🥎   When the catcher is making a **PLAY** on a base **RUNNER.**

EFFECT / PENALTY

1st Offense (all codes): When the catcher violates this provision, a **BALL** shall be awarded to the **BATTER**. In **NCAA**, the catcher is also warned.
2nd Offense (NCAA only): Catcher is ejected after being warned.

Note: *NCAA and ASA provide exceptions if ANY base runners are on. The catcher may throw to ANY base, even if empty, provided there are other base runners. However for NFHS, the catcher MUST be making a play on an actual base runner. Otherwise the penalty would be imposed.*

NFHS rules do not permit a team to circumvent the requirement of actually throwing "four-pitches" to intentionally walk a batter. In this case, the umpire will not issue a ball on the batter, as this benefits the defensive team and puts the batter at a disadvantage.

Rules Reference
USSSA 6.2B / NFHS 6-3-2 / ASA 6-7B / NCAA 10.16, 11.3.2.5

CHARGED CONFERENCES

A conference is **CHARGED** (and documented) whenever a **COACH** (or bench personnel) requests and is granted time-out to meet with a defensive or offensive player.

- All conferences should be **RECORDED** by the home plate umpire.

- Time out requested for attending to an **INJURED PLAYER** does **NOT COUNT,** provided no coaching occurs while dealing with the injured player.

- The charged conference rule applies once the **BALL** becomes **LIVE** to start an inning.

Umpires should alert the coach if a time out is being charged to avoid potential problems later in the game. If excessive time outs are requested they should be denied by the umpire to prevent additional penalties.

Rules Reference
USSSA 4.8 / NFHS 4-7; POE #3 / ASA 5-7; RS #9 / NCAA 6.11.4; 6.11.5

CHARGED CONFERENCE (OFFENSE)

OFFENSIVE CONFERENCES	USSSA	NFHS	ASA	NCAA
Recorded by Plate Umpire	Plate Umpire Records All Charged Conferences			
Maximum Number	Once Ball Becomes Live - Offensive Conferences are Charged with Maximum of <u>ONE</u> per inning.			
Extra Inning Allowance	Teams are Permitted <u>ONE</u> Additional Charged Conference in Each Extra Inning			
Request for Excessive Conference	Umpire Should DENY Requests for Excessive Charged Conferences Beyond <u>ONE</u> per Inning			
Excess Results In Additional Penalty		Coach Restriction to Bench		Team Representative(s) or Player(s) who initiate are ejected
Conferring with Base Runners, On-Deck, and Current Batter	Coaches are Permitted to Confer with Players and Must Resume Play when Directed by the Umpire			
Opposing Team Able to Huddle During Charged Conference	Provided they are Ready to Play when Umpire is Ready to Resume Play after Charged Conference			
Opposing Team is ALSO Charged	Opposing Team is ALSO Charged (Conference) if they are Not Ready to Play when the Umpire Directs Play to Resume			
Offensive Team Huddles on Field While Defense is Warming Up Between Innings	No Reference	Not Permitted	No Reference	

Rules Reference
USSSA 4.8 / NFHS 4-7; POE #3 / ASA 5-7a / NCAA 6.11.5

CHARGED CONFERENCE (DEFENSE)

DEFENSIVE CONFERENCES	USSSA	NFHS	ASA	NCAA
Recorded by Plate Umpire	*Plate Umpire Records All Charged Conference* *			
Maximum Per Game	*THREE per Regulation Game*			
Maximum Per Inning				*ONE* ** per Inning
Extra Innings	Receive **ONE** Extra Conference per each Extra Inning			
Excess Effect	*Excess Charged Time Out Results in Removal of Pitcher as Pitcher*			*Deny Request*
Excess Results in Removal / Ejection				Team Representative(s) or Player(s) who initiate are ejected
Opposing Team Able to Huddle During Charged Conference	*Provided they are Ready to Play when Umpire is Ready to Resume Play after Charged Conference*			
Opposing Team Able to Huddle During Catcher/Pitcher Conference	*Provided they are Ready to Play when Umpire is Ready to Resume Play after Catcher/Pitcher Conference*			
No Conference Charged *	*Removal of Pitcher Does NOT Count as a Charged Conference* **			
Pitcher Substitutions	*Umpire must be Notified on Pitching Changes / Substitutions*			

*NFHS / ASA: It is **NOT** a charged conference if the coach talks to a pitcher before removing her as a pitcher. USSSA / NCAA: It is a **CHARGED** conference if the coach either steps over the foul line or consults with another player **PRIOR** to informing the umpire of the pitching change.*

 NCAA: An additional defensive conference is permitted for each **NEW PITCHER entering the game in that half inning. Base runners are not restricted to their bases during warm-up pitches. Runners are only restricted during suspension of play for the administration of a substitution.*

Rules Reference
USSSA 4.8; Case p 12 / NFHS 3-7-1; 4-7; POE #3 / ASA 5-7b / NCAA 6.11.4

CHECKED SWING

To be a **CHECKED SWING** the following observations must be made by the home plate (and base) umpire(s):

- The batter must attempt to **RESTRAIN** the bat from hitting the ball during an attempted hit, slap or bunting.

- The barrel of the **BAT** should **NOT** be carried in front of the batter's body in the direction of the infield.

The plate umpire makes the **INITIAL DETERMINATION** whether the batter **CHECKED** her swing or **STRUCK** completely at the ball.

Once the plate umpire determines the batter **SWUNG** at the ball, this decision in **NOT REVERSIBLE** by a team appealing for help.

If the plate umpire has ruled the batter **CHECKED** her swing, a player or coach **MAY** request the plate umpire for **HELP** from the base umpire, if they are in proper position.

In **NCAA** games, the plate umpire **MUST** request help from the appropriate base umpire if requested by the catcher after the pitch is ruled a ball.

The final decision should be based on whether the batter actually **STRUCK** at the **BALL.**

In games where the two umpire system is used, the base umpire may NOT be in a good position to assist on "checked swing" calls at the plate. In these cases coaches should realize the plate umpire must bear the burden of determining if the batter swung fully on the pitch.

Rules Reference
USSSA 14.8 Note / NFHS 2-11; 10-1-4N / ASA RS-10 / NCAA 11.12

COLLAPSIBLE FENCES

Facilities that utilize collapsible fences are becoming more popular today. These temporary structures can flex and fold down to prevent injury of a fielder attempting to make a catch.

Here are some guidelines to remember as it relates to a collapsible fence and a legal catch.

For **USSSA**, **NFHS**, and **NCAA**:

- The fielder may **CONTACT** the fence while attempting to make a legal catch.

- The fielder may place **ONE FOOT** (or **BOTH** feet) on the fence which may **DISPLACE** the fence from a vertical position toward a more horizontal position.

- Contacting the ball (during the catch) while the **FENCE** is **FLEXING** or being displaced is perfectly legal – provided the touching of the ball is **PRIOR** to the fence being **FULLY DISPLACED** or lying **FLAT** on the ground.

- If the fence is **ALREADY LYING FLAT / HORIZONTAL** and the fielder makes contact with the ball, **NO LEGAL CATCH** can be made. In the case of a fly ball a home run would be awarded.

ASA does not have these same restrictions. A fielder may stand on a fallen portable fence and make a legal catch.

Rules Reference
USSSA 3.15 / NFHS 9-2-7 / ASA Rule Supplement 20; Casebook 1-15/ NCAA 9.2.7

COURTESY RUNNERS

All codes (**<u>except NCAA</u>**) **PERMIT** the use of an **OPTIONAL** courtesy runner. The pitcher or catcher is **<u>NOT</u>** required to leave the game when a courtesy runner is used.

REQUIREMENTS	USSSA	NFHS	ASA	NCAA
May Use A Courtesy Runner for Pitcher or Catcher	*Permitted for Either at Anytime They Reach Base Optional Choice and Not Mandatory*			
Who is Eligible ?	*Any Eligible Substitute Who is NOT in the Game Can Be Used as a Courtesy Runner*			
Last Recorded Out Can Be Courtesy Runner	*Not Permitted*			
Once Player Participates in Game	*They are Ineligible to be a Courtesy Runner*			*Courtesy Runners are NOT Permitted in NCAA Play*
Pitcher / Catcher May Return to Run for Courtesy Runner	*If Runner is Injured*	*If Runner is Injured or DQ'd*	*Not Permitted*	
Same Player May NOT Run for BOTH Pitcher AND Catcher	*Not in Same Inning*	*Not in Same Game*	*Not in Same Inning or Game*	
Courtesy Runner Can Become Substitute	*Not in Same Half Inning Unless Injury and No Substitute is Available*			
Courtesy Runner for Another Courtesy Runner	*Only if Injury*	*Not Permitted*		

(Continued on Next Page)

COURTESY RUNNERS
(Continued)

If a team is using a Designated Player **(DP)** and the **(DP)** is batting only (not playing defense for the pitcher / catcher) they are **NOT** permitted to have a courtesy runner.

Courtesy Runners are not permitted if a **(DP)** or Designated Hitter **(DH)** is batting only and **NOT** playing defense for the pitcher/catcher.

USSSA permits a courtesy runner to become a substitute in the same half inning if injury forces a team to play short-handed. If a courtesy runner is used in the first half inning for the starting pitcher or catcher who does not pitch (or catch) to start the first inning then the player who was a courtesy runner is considered a substitute.

Although Courtesy Runners are **NOT** considered substitutes, they **MUST** be reported to the umpire before entering the game.

Failure for a coach to **REPORT** a courtesy runner carries additional penalties based on the appropriate code:

- **USSSA**: Unreported Substitute Penalty.
- **NFHS**: Unreported Substitute Penalty.
- **ASA**: Illegal Runner (Player DQ'd).
- **NCAA:** Courtesy Runners are <u>NOT</u> permitted at any time.

(See Appropriate Section for Additional Penalties)

Rules Reference
USSSA 8.3 / NFHS 8-9 / ASA 8-10

DOUBLE BASES

Using a **DOUBLE FIRST BASE** the following applies:

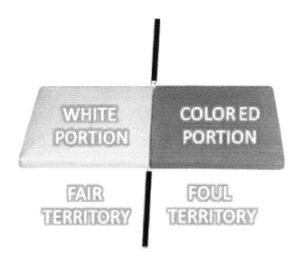

ASA: Double bases shall be used for **ALL LEVELS** of play.
NCAA: Use of a double base is **NOT** permitted.
NFHS: Permitted by State Adoption.
USSSA: Permitted but not mandatory.

The **DEFENSE MUST** use the **WHITE** portion and the **BATTER-RUNNER MUST** use the **COLORED** portion of the base when a **PLAY** is being made on the batter-runner.

Color: Must be Orange (USSSA) or contrasting for NFHS and ASA.

The batter-runner can be called **OUT** when a play is being made and they touch the **WHITE** portion **ONLY**. This is considered over running first base and the defense must **APPEAL** before the batter-runner returns to touch **EITHER** portion of the base.

The batter-runner (or any runner) **MAY USE** the **WHITE** or **COLORED** portion of the base while **ADVANCING** on balls hit to the **OUTFIELD** while no plays are being attempted on the base, while **RETURNING** to first base, while **TAGGING UP** to advance on a fly ball, or returning to the base on an attempted **PICK OFF**. The **DEFENSE** may also use **BOTH** portions on these plays or appeals.

(Continued on Next Page)

DOUBLE BASES
(Continued)

INTERFERENCE is called when a collision occurs during a force play and the batter-runner touches **ONLY** the **WHITE** portion of the base.

OBSTRUCTION (Delayed Dead Ball) is ruled when a collision occurs during a force play and the fielder (along with the batter-runner) is touching the **COLORED** portion of the base **ONLY**.

The **DEFENSE** and the **BATTER-RUNNER** may use **BOTH PORTIONS** of the base on force-out attempts from the foul side of the base, or on errant throws that pull the fielder into foul ground.

 *Umpires, coaches, and captains should discuss the use of a double first base during the pre-game conference if they are unfamiliar with its use.*

Rules Reference
USSSA 8.19 / NFHS 8-10 / ASA 2-3h; 8-2M / NCAA 2.4

DP / FLEX GUIDELINES

The **DESIGNATED PLAYER (DP) / FLEX** Rule provides flexibility for athlete participation under **USSSA, NFHS, ASA and NCAA** rules.

By choice **PRIOR** to the start of a game,

- A team may start with **nine or ten** players as submitted in the official lineup.
- If they **start with nine**, they can **never increase to ten**.
- If they **start with ten** (using the DP), they can, at any time, **reduce to nine** and/or increase **back to ten**.
- Under certain circumstances, they may **end the game with nine or ten** in the lineup.
- The role of the **DP is never terminated** by rule.

NO.		PLAYER	RE	POS.
19	1	HARRIS		6
	SUB.			
17	2	ABLE		4
	SUB.			
20	3	THOMAS		8
	SUB.			
24	4	JONES		DP
	SUB.			
15	5	ALEXANDER		3
	SUB.			
22	6	MOORE		2
	SUB.			
25	7	COOPER		7
	SUB.			
7	8	MORRIS		5
	SUB.			
3	9	RODGERS		1
	SUB.			
18	10	GREEN (FLEX)		9
	SUB.			

NO.	SUBSTITUTES	POS.
10	HOWELL	
4	BAKER	
6	SMITH	

A **designated player (DP) may bat for any defensive player** (in the field) provided it is made known prior to the start of the game. Once designated to bat for a player, the DP can bat only for that player and any substitutes for that player. They are sometimes referred to as twins ... the player/twin for whom the DP is hitting (FLEX) must be listed in 10th position of the lineup.

- The DP position, if used, must be **indicated in the batting order** as one of the **nine batting positions**.
- Like all starting players, the DP and the FLEX, may **reenter the game** one time provided it is in their **original position** in the batting order.
- All players, including the DP and the FLEX, must **leave and reenter** the game from their **original spot** in the lineup.
  (Note: The FLEX may bat or run in the DP's spot in the batting order.)
- **Substitutes** for the DP and the FLEX, must be recorded and **tracked in** that player's **original spot** in the lineup similar to any other player.
- **USSSA** utilizes "Additional Players" (AP) as well. AP's must bat and are considered in the lineup, just like the DP. AP's can play defense as well. If playing for the FLEX the FLEX is considered to have left the game, and the lineup is reduced by one.

(continued on next page)

About the Designated Player (DP)

- The DP **must play offense** to be in the game.
- The DP can **never play defense only**.
- The DP **may play defense for any player** in the lineup **or** for the FLEX.

If the **DP plays defense for any player** in the lineup (besides the FLEX):

- That player becomes a **batter only**.
  (NCAA designates this person the Offensive Player or "OP")
- She continues to **bat in her same position** in the lineup.
- Has **not left the game** as the team is still playing with ten.

If the **DP plays defense** for the FLEX:

- The **FLEX** has left the game.
- The team is now playing with **NINE**.

*The DP may be replaced as a batter (or runner) by a substitute **or** by the FLEX. When this situation happens, the DP has left the game and must reenter (if eligible) in order to be in the game again. If the DP is replaced by a substitute, that substitute becomes the DP and has all the privileges of the DP position. The team is playing with ten players.*

If the **DP is replaced by** the FLEX:

- The **FLEX** is now playing both offense **and** defense.
- The team is now playing with only **NINE** players.
- The **DP** (or the DP's substitute) and the **FLEX** can never play offense at the same time.

(continued on next page)

About the FLEX

By rule, the **FLEX** must play defense to be considered in the game. Also consider...

- The **FLEX** can never play offense only.
- The **FLEX** can play any defensive position.
- The **FLEX** may only play offense for the **DP** in the **DP's** position in the lineup.

If the **FLEX plays offense** for the DP, the **DP has now left the game** and the team is **playing with nine**. Also, the **FLEX may be replaced on defense** by a substitute or by the DP. When this happens the **FLEX has left the game** and must reenter (if eligible) in order to be in the game again.

If the **FLEX is replaced** by a legal <u>**substitute**</u>:
- That substitute becomes the **FLEX** and has all the privileges of the **FLEX** position.
- The team is now playing with **TEN** players.

If the **FLEX is replaced** by the <u>**DP**</u> :
- The **DP** is playing both offense and defense and the team is playing with only **NINE** players.
- The **FLEX** and the **FLEX's** substitute can never play defense at the same time.

 *Remember... The FLEX and the DP **<u>can</u> play defense** at the **same time**. For this to occur the DP must be playing defense for another player in the lineup and not for the FLEX.*

(continued on next page)

Situations Involving the DP / FLEX

If the **FLEX** is playing offense for the **DP** and the **DP** reenters, or a substitute for the **DP** enters or re-enters:

- The **FLEX** player can return to the number **10** position and play defense only, or...
- The **FLEX** can leave the game if the **DP** (or a substitute) is going to play defense for her.

If the **DP** is playing defense for the **FLEX** and the **FLEX** reenters, or a substitute for the **FLEX** enters or reenters:

- The **DP** can remain in the **DP** position in the lineup and play offense only, or ...
- The **DP** can play defense for another player in the lineup, or...
- The **DP** can leave the game if the **FLEX** is going to play offense for her.

Placing the **FLEX** player into the first nine positions in the lineup for a player <u>other than</u> the **DP** is:

- Considered an **illegal** substitution.
- The illegal substitute (the **FLEX**) shall be **removed** (NCAA= ejected) from the game.
- The illegal substitute shall be **restricted** to the dugout/bench.

Any other infraction involving the **DP** or the **FLEX** player is a violation of the substitution rule, the re-entry rule, or the batting out of order rule.

For more information on the DP/FLEX visit:
bluebook60.com

Download a <u>FREE</u> iTunes Audio Podcast on "Understanding the DP / FLEX"
Search the iTunes Store with keywords: "softball DP FLEX"

Rules Reference
USSSA 3.23, 3.29, 5.1, 5.4 / NFHS 2-54, 2-57-1, 3-1-1, 3-3-2, 3-3-6 / ASA 4.3 / NCAA 8.2

EJECTIONS – WHERE DO THEY GO?

PLAYERS after an ejection must comply with the following:

- ⚾ **ASA**: Must **LEAVE** the **GROUNDS** and provide **NO CONTACT** with umpires or other participants.
- ⚾ **NFHS / USSSA**: Players are **RESTRICTED** to the **DUGOUT** to maintain proper supervision by coaching staff.
- ⚾ **NCAA**: May **REMAIN** in the **DUGOUT** but **CANNOT COMMUNICATE** with opponents or umpires. Subsequent violations shall result in a game forfeit.

NON-PLAYING PERSONNEL after an ejection must comply with the following:

- ⚾ **USSSA/ASA**: Must **LEAVE** the **GROUNDS** and provide **NO CONTACT** with umpires or other participants. There is no mention of identifying an alternative head coach to continue the game.
- ⚾ **NFHS**: Must **LEAVE** the **VICINITY** and is prohibited contact with either team.
- ⚾ **NCAA**: Must **LEAVE** the playing **FIELD** and **DUGOUT**. They may leave the grounds but if they **REMAIN**, they must move to a location near or behind the **OUTFIELD FENCE** between the foul poles or leave the complex and be out of sight and sound. They also may not communicate further with teams or umpires.
- ⚾ **NCAA**: If the **HEAD COACH** is **EJECTED**, the plate umpire shall ask for identification of the acting head coach replacement. If the head coach refuses to identify the replacement a game forfeit shall be ruled.

Rules Reference
USSSA 12.1 / NFHS 3-6-20 / ASA 4-8-B / NCAA 13.2

ELECTRONIC EQUIPMENT

The use of electronic equipment which includes **CELL PHONES, RADIOS, iPADS, COMPUTERS**, etc... have restrictions on the playing field (and dugout) based on the various rule codes.

USSSA:

- Electronic equipment **MAY NOT** be used for **COACHING** purposes. Wristband (Play Indicators) are considered legal for players and coaches.
- Coaches **MAY** use electronic aids (iPads, laptops, etc) as a scoring device.

NFHS:

- The use of electronic devices **IS PERMITTED** by team personnel in dugout only. However any information obtained shall not be used to review decisions made by the umpires.
- **PARENTS** are permitted to video tape and give to the coach but it must be used in the dugout only. No team personnel shall video tape outside of dugout.

ASA:

- No electronic equipment may be **WORN** or **CARRIED** on to the field.
- After a **WARNING**, the offending player / coach is ejected.

NCAA:

- Cell phones are **NOT PERMITTED** on the **PLAYING FIELD**.
- Cell phones **ARE** **PERMITTED** in the **DUGOUT** provided they are **NOT** used for **COACHING** or scouting purposes.
- After a **WARNING** the offender is ejected if not immediately compliant with the request.
- Only non-uniformed personnel are permitted to be **OUTSIDE** the **TEAM AREAS** for purposes of videotaping, recording pitch speeds, running a scoreboard, etc.

*For **NCAA** contests, both players and non-players become ineligible to participate in the game if they are videotaping. For example, if a coach is videotaping while his team is on defense, they cannot come to the field and coach first base when on offense.*

Rules Reference
USSSA 11.2F / NFHS, 3-6-11 / ASA 4-7-C5 / NCAA 5.9

ERASING CHALK LINES

NFHS and NCAA: Players, coaches, and bench personnel are **NOT PERMITTED to INTENTIONALLY** erase chalk lines within the **BATTER'S BOX** <u>or</u> on the **FIELD** of **PLAY**.

- A **STRIKE** is given to the batter if the batter or any member of the **OFFENSE TEAM INTENTIONALLY** erases a line.

- A **BALL** is awarded to the batter if the catcher or any member of the **DEFENSIVE TEAM INTENTIONALLY** erases a line.

NFHS

- NFHS requires after awarding the appropriate **BALL** or **STRIKE** for erasing a line, the offending team shall be **ISSUED** a **WARNING**.
- Any **SUBSEQUENT** violations will result in the offender **AND** head coach being **RESTRICTED** to the **BENCH** for the remainder of the game.

NCAA

- **SUBSEQUENT** violations by the same team shall result in the violator's **EJECTION**.
- Intentionally erasing the **PITCHER'S LANE** line shall result in a violation.

ASA and USSSA
No specific provision regarding the removal of chalk lines.

__Rules Reference__
NFHS 3-6-17 / NCAA 2.16

EQUIPMENT VERIFICATION & MISUSE

For a **NFHS and ASA** game it should be noted that the contest may **NOT BEGIN** until the **HEAD COACH** attends the pre-game conference.

In **USSSA**, the head coach must be identified and one adult coach must attend the pre-game conference. **NCAA** requires one member of the coaching staff to attend the conference and identify the official scorer. Players and/or designated captains may attend but are not required to do so.

During the pre-game conference the following may be discussed:
- Head coach (or **USSSA** adult coach attending conference) **VERIFIES** that all players are equipped properly. (Except **NCAA** – not necessary)
- Their **EQUIPMENT** is **LEGAL** – as requested by the home plate umpire. (**NFHS Only**)

For **NFHS** if **ILLEGAL EQUIPMENT** is **DISCOVERED** in the game after the coach has provided their verification it shall be removed or made legal. This also results in a:
- Team Warning Issued and ...
- The next offense will result in the head coach and offender being restricted to the bench for the remainder of the game.

BANGING of **BATS** in the dugout to generate noise is considered "misuse" of equipment. All codes **PROHIBIT** the misuse of equipment and using it in a way it was not intended to be used. Banging of bats is specifically prohibited and should be considered an unsportsmanlike act by the offending team. Additionally the **BANGING** of **SOFTBALLS** inside the dugout in a rhythmic pattern should be prohibited for the same reason (In NCAA only when brought to the attention of the umpire).

Rules Reference
USSSA 5.8D / NFHS 3-5-1; 3-6-1 /ASA Interpretations / NCAA 3.1.2

FORFEIT SITUATIONS

Team(s) **FAILURE TO APPEAR** on Field:

- **USSSA / ASA**: A forfeit is declared.
  Refer to Umpire in Chief or Tournament Director.
- **NFHS**: By state adoption and varies.
- **NCAA**: This is not a forfeit but rather a "No-Contest" which is declared.

Team(s) **REFUSE** to **BEGIN / CONTINUE** Game:

- **USSSA**: Forfeit after 1 minute of waiting after warning.
- **NFHS**: By state adoption. May be a forfeit if team refuses to play or if a team delays greater than 1 minute after the umpire directs the team to "play ball."
- **ASA**: Forfeit after the proper time as indicated by the tournament association.
- **NCAA**: Forfeit declared 5 minutes after the umpire has directed teams to "play ball" at the beginning of the game or during the game if one side refuses to play. If after play has been suspended by the umpire one team refuses to play after 2 minutes, a forfeit shall be declared.

After **EJECTION:**

- **USSSA, NFHS,** and **ASA**: Forfeit if order not obeyed within 1 minute of umpires direction. Also if the number of players remaining will be below the required minimum.
- **NCAA**: Forfeit is not obeyed in a timely manner and a final "60 second" warning is issued and elapsed. Also if the number of players remaining is less than 9.

Who **DECLARES** Forfeit?

- **USSSA / NFHS**: The plate umpire (umpire in chief) has the sole responsibility.
- **ASA**: Both the plate and base umpires have equal authority.
- **NCAA**: All umpires must concur in order to declare a forfeit.

Rules Reference
USSSA 4.7; 14.12L / NFHS 4-3-1; 10-2-2 / ASA 5.4; Man p221/ NCAA 6.3.3, 6.19

GAME LIMITS (MISCELLANEOUS)

RUN AHEAD / FORFEIT				
	USSSA	NFHS	ASA	NCAA
After 5 or More Complete Innings (or 4 ½ with Home Ahead)	8 Runs Ahead	By State Adoption	8 Runs Ahead	8 Runs Ahead
After 4 Complete Innings (or 3 ½ with Home Ahead)	10 Runs Ahead	By State Adoption	12 Runs Ahead	
After 3 Complete Innings (or 2 ½ with Home Ahead)	12 Runs Ahead		15 Runs Ahead	
International Tie Breaker Starts	To Start 8th Inning or After Time Limit	By State Adoption	To Start 8th Inning or After Time Limit	May be used in 10th Inning by Conference or Tournament Policy. Discussed in Pre-Game
Game Can End in Tie	During Pool Play	By State Adoption	Not Permitted in Tournament Play -- Stopped Tie Games Resume from Point of Interruption	Considered Regulation Tie Game. Leagues may use Halted Game Rule to Finish at Point of Interruption
Who Declares a Forfeit (or Termination) If Neccessary	Tourney Director Only	Plate Umpire Only	Plate or Base Umpire(s)	All Umpires Must Concur
Forfeited / Terminated Game Score	7 - 0 in Favor of the Team Not at Fault			

Prudent umpires should continually encourage the two teams' scorekeepers to verify the run count and innings are correct after each full inning. Additionally the plate (or base) umpire may keep track (separately) of this information as a third check point during the game.

Rules Reference
USSSA 4.4; 4.5; 4.7 / NFHS 4-2-3, 5&6 / ASA 5-9-A1; 5-11; 5-3
NCAA 6.13; 6.14, 6.15, 6.19

GLOVE REQUIREMENTS

Illegal gloves, when discovered, shall be **REMOVED** immediately from the **GAME** by the umpire.

All fielders **MUST** wear a **MITT** <u>or</u> **GLOVE**. The **CATCHER'S MITT** may be **ANY** size. Gloves may not contain **TACKY** or **STICKY** substances.

NFHS / ASA / USSSA: Gloves may be a **MAXIMUM TWO COLORS** and **LACING** is not considered one of the colors. The umpire may deem any glove's **COLORS** to be distracting and request removal.

Gloves that are entirely **OPTIC (YELLOW/GREEN)** or **COLOR** of the **BALL** are **ILLEGAL COLORS** and not permissible. Any attachments, printing, designs or optic markings that resemble the **APPEARANCE OF A SOFTBALL** or deemed **DISTRACTING** may be considered **ILLEGAL**.

NCAA: GLOVES may be **ANY COLOR** or combination of colors **EXCEPT** the color of the ball.

The **HEIGHT** of the glove (from heel to highest point) shall **NOT EXCEED 14 INCHES**.

The **WIDTH** of the glove (from the webbing farthest from the thumb to the outside of the little finger) shall **NOT EXCEED 8 INCHES**.

The **WEBBING** shall **NOT EXCEED 5¾ INCHES (NCAA shall not exceed 5")**.

See **GLOVE- ILLEGAL USE** (next page) for penalties when detected.

*Any fielder is permitted to utilize a **MITT** (first base style or catcher) while playing **ANY** position if it meets all specifications to be legal*

Rules Reference
USSSA 2.9 / NFHS 1-4; 8-8-15 / ASA 3-4 / NCAA 3.6

GLOVE – ILLEGAL USE

USSSA, NFHS, and ASA: When a player uses an **ILLEGAL GLOVE** and it is brought to the attention of the umpire a **DELAY DEAD BALL** is ruled. For **NCAA**, **TIME** is called and the glove is removed.

When **NO PLAY** is made by the defensive player wearing the **ILLEGAL GLOVE**:

The glove shall be **REMOVED** from the game **IMMEDIATELY**.

If the player **TOUCHED / PLAYED** a **LIVE BALL** with the **ILLEGAL GLOVE** and it is detected:

- ⚾ **BEFORE** the next **LEGAL** or **ILLEGAL PITCH**.
- ⚾ **BEFORE** the **PITCHER** and all **INFIELDERS** have left fair territory and the **CATCHER** left her position.
- ⚾ **BEFORE** the **UMPIRES** have **LEFT** the field.

The **OFFENDED** team's coach has several **OPTIONS**:

- ⚾ The offensive team can **CHOOSE** to take the **RESULT** of the play and disregard the illegal act.
- ⚾ The offensive coach may choose to **NULLIFY** the entire play with all **RUNNERS RETURNING** to original positions at the "time of pitch." The batter shall **BAT OVER** again with the **SAME** ball/strike **COUNT** prior to the play.
- ⚾ **USSSA**: Awards 3 bases for touching a batted ball, 2 bases for touching a thrown ball, or 4 bases if prevented ball from going over fence.

Rules Reference
USSSA 8.14; 10.4f / NFHS 8-8-15 / ASA 8-8o; RS #23 / NCAA 3.6 (Effect)

HELMET REQUIREMENTS

All **PLAYERS MUST** wear an approved protective batting helmet while at **BAT**, **RUNNING** the bases and while **COACHING** bases.

Batting Helmet Requirements	USSSA	NFHS	ASA	NCAA
Face Guard Required	✔	✔	✔	Optional
NOCSAE Seal Visible	Must be Visible			
Warning Lable Visible	Must be on Shell or Under Bill			
Catcher's Helmet Double Flaps	Required for Catchers			
Base Coaches on Field	Non Adult / Student Coaches Must Wear Helmet while On-Field and in Coaching Boxes			
Intentionally Removing Helmet on Field During LIVE Ball (First Violation)	Warning to Offending Player and Coach		Player is Out based on Umpire Discretion	Failure when directed by Umpire results in Player Ejection. Intentionally removing results in player declared out.
Intentionally Removing Helmet on Field During LIVE Ball (Second Violation)	Player Restricted to Bench and Coach Ejected			
Defensive Helmets Permitted	Optional	Non-Glare Only	Must Be Team Hat Color	Optional, but all same color.

NCAA and NFHS have banned the use of highly reflective (mirror-like) surfaces on helmets. NFHS requires catcher eye shields to be non-reflective and clear.

NCAA Note: Double Flaps are not a requirement for Catchers.

All Codes require the use of a Protective Face Mask for Catchers.

Rules Reference
USSSA 2.1, 2.2 / NFHS 1-6-6 & 8; 1-7-1, 1-8-4 / ASA 3-5A,C,& E / NCAA 3.7

INTERFERENCE DEFINED

Interference is when the **OFFENSE** illegally **IMPEDES**, **HINDERS**, or **CONFUSES** a fielder. This can be **PHYSICALLY** or **VERBALLY** and can also involve an umpire, spectator, or even equipment.

- **ALL CODES (Except NCAA)**: Interference (unlike obstruction) causes the ball to become **DEAD** immediately when it occurs.

- Contact is **NOT** always necessary to have interference.

- Malicious contact by a runner on a fielder (with or without the ball – in or out of the baseline) is **ALWAYS** interference.

ALL CODES (Except NCAA): When a player (batter or runner) causes interference, they are declared **OUT** and other runners must return to bases last legally occupied at the time of the infraction. If a runner causes the interference the batter is awarded first base.

NCAA (New for 2016-17): Interference by the **BATTER** causes the umpire to rule a **DELAYED DEAD BALL.** The defensive team shall choose either the **RESULT OF THE PLAY** or the **BATTER** is declared **OUT** and runners must **RETURN** to their last base occupied (at the time of pitch or when the interference occurred) depending on the type of interference. See NCAA Rules: 11.21

 *When interference is caused by a **RETIRED BATTER** or **RUNNER** additional penalties are imposed based on specific codes.*

*(See separate section on "**Interference by a Retired Player**")*

Rules Reference
USSSA 3.39 / NFHS 2-32 / ASA Rule 1 and RS #33 / NCAA 11.19-11.22

INTERFERENCE BY THE BATTER

The **BATTER** (or sometimes runner) is declared **OUT** if the batter actively (or intentionally) hinders/interferes with the catcher (or another fielder) making a play on a base runner.

CAUSE	EFFECT			
	USSSA	NFHS	ASA	NCAA
Batter Intentionally Interferes with Catcher	*STANDARD EFFECT (Except NCAA)*			
Interfering by Leaning Over Home Plate	*The Ball is Dead – The Batter is Declared Out Runners Return to the Last Base Legally Occupied Prior to the Interference*			
Hinder Action/Throw Around Home Plate				
Failure to Vacate a Crowded Plate Area	*NCAA EFFECT – see below***			
Batter Switches Batter's Boxes when Pitcher is in Position and Ready to Pitch	*Ball is Dead and Batter is Out for Disconcerting Pitcher - Runners Must Return* **			
Batter Interference on Play at Plate with TWO OUTS	*STANDARD EFFECT - Batter is Out - 3rd Out of Inning* **			
Batter Interference on Play at Plate with LESS THAN TWO OUTS	*STANDARD EFFECT*			*Runner is Declared Out* **
Catcher's Throw Accidently Hits Batter or Batter's Bat	*Ignored*	*Ignored Unless Batter Re-Establishes Position**	*Ignored Unless Batter is OUT of Box*	***In Box**: Ignore Unless Intentional* ***Out of Box** is Interference* **

NFHS Note: Ignore if catcher's throw accidently hits the batter while standing in the box. But if the batter moves and re-establishes position after the catcher controls the ball and is attempting to throw, then this would be considered interference.

**NCAA Note (New 2016-17): Delayed dead ball is signaled. The defensive team shall choose either the result of the play---- or the batter is out and each base runner must return to the base legally occupied at the time of the pitch or time of interference based on the type of interference. See 11.21

Rules Reference
USSSA 3.39 / NFHS 2-32; 7-4-4a / ASA Rule 1 and RS #33 / NCAA 11.19-11.22

INTERFERENCE BY THE BATTER RUNNER

CAUSE	EFFECT			
	USSSA	NFHS	ASA	NCAA
Running After a Dropped Third Strike (Entitled to Run)	Interference only if batter-runner violates the running lane provisions.**			
Running After a Dropped Third Stirke (Not Entitled to Run)	Interference and Runner Closest to Home is Declared Out	No Interference		Interference and Runner Closest to Home is Declared Out
Intentionally Interfering with a FOUL Ground Ball	Not Interference - Must Be Fair	Interference if Umpire Judges Ball Could be Fair	Not Interference - Must Be Fair	Interference - Batter is Out
Running Lane: Throw Hits Batter-Runner with One Foot IN and One Foot OUT	If either foot is on GROUND and OUTSIDE lane when player is hit - she is declared OUT.		Depends on Area of Body Hit in Reference to Lane	Runner's Lane Removed**
Ball Hits Batter-Runner After Infield Fly Rule	Dead Ball (Interference) - Runners Return and Runner Closest to Home is Declared Out.		Interference - Runners Return	Same as USSSA and NFHS.

NCAA Note: If the batter (not entitled to run to first base) prevents the catcher from attempting a pick-off play by running toward first base in fair territory the runner closest to home will be declared out. Interference must be ruled.

****NCAA (New 2016-17):** Runner's Lane (Chalk) Line is removed. This only changes the look of the field but has no effect on the batter-runner's responsibility to not interfere with the fielder receiving the throw at first base and she still cannot deviate from her basepath nor move backward if a fielder is attempting a tag play.

Rules Reference
USSSA 8.18 / NFHS 8-1, 8-2, 5-1.1e / ASA 8-2 / NCAA 11.19-11.22

INTERFERENCE BY THE RUNNER

A **RUNNER** (or batter-runner) that interferes with a fielder executing an **INITIAL PLAY** causes the ball to become **DEAD** immediately.

Consider the following:

Determination must be made whether the interference occurred **BEFORE** or **AFTER** the runner was declared **OUT** if a play is being made on her.

(See separate section on "Interference by a Retired Player")

Interference occurs if a runner is hit with a **BATTED BALL** before it passes an infielder (other than the pitcher.)

A deflected ball hitting a runner is **NOT** interference, if **NO OTHER PLAYER** has an opportunity to make an initial play on the ball.

Runner must **VACATE** (or provide sufficient) space a fielder needs to make a play on a ball – except for the legally occupied base.

ASA: On a **FOUL FLY BALL** that (in the umpire's judgment) could have been caught with ordinary effort, and interference occurs, **BOTH** the **RUNNER** and **BATTER** are declared **OUT**. Otherwise, the ball is dead and a strike is awarded to the batter.

 *Interference (when called) will automatically cause the ball to become dead IMMEDIATELY**. Runners are not permitted to advance after interference is ruled on a runner.*

**NCAA Exception: When interference is caused by the batter then a delayed dead ball is ruled.

(Continued on Next Page)

INTERFERENCE BY THE RUNNER
(Continued)

If a runner is off the base and struck by a declared **INFIELD FLY**, both the runner and batter are declared out. If two runners are struck by the same fair ball, only the first runner is declared out.

CAUSE	EFFECT			
	USSSA	**NFHS**	**ASA**	**NCAA**
Interfere with Fielder Attempting to Field FAIR FLY Ball	*No Difference Between Ground/Fly Ball - Runner is Declared Out - Batter Awarded First Base*		*If Prevents Fielder from Catching Fly Ball - Runner AND Batter are Declared Out.*	
Interfere with Fielder Attempting to Field FOUL FLY Ball	*Runner is Out and Foul Ball is Declared on the Batter. If a Bunt after 2 strikes, Batter is Declared Out.*		*Batter AND Runner are Declared Out*	*Same as USSSA and NFHS.*
Interfere with Fielder Attempting to Play Deflected Ball Off Other Fielder	*Interference if Intentional or for NFHS, deflecting off Pitcher.*			
Double Play Attempt and Non-Retired Runner	*Runner Closest to Home is Declared Out*	*Succeeding Runner is Declared Out*		*Runner Being Played on is Declared*

 *If a fly ball is hit "into" a dugout area and the defender reaches into **dead ball area** to make a catch, (USSSA, NFHS, and ASA) deem it can be ruled interference, provided an offensive team member actually interferes. However for NCAA, there is no interference if the player is prevented from catching the ball by the player on the bench.*

Rules Reference
USSSA 8.18F,G&H / NFHS 7-4-4, 2-47-3, 8-6-10a / ASA 7-6p; 8-2F3; 8-7 / NCAA 12.19

INTERFERENCE: BALL TOUCHES RUNNER ON BASE

When a fair **BATTED** ball **TOUCHES** a runner who is in **CONTACT** with a **BASE,** the following must be considered:

- Runners on a legally occupied base are **NOT PERMITTED** to **INTENTIONALLY** hinder a fielder.
- Runners are also **NOT REQUIRED** to vacate that base.

ALL CODES:

- Ball is **LIVE** if the closest fielder is in **FRONT** of the **BASE.**
- Ball is **DEAD** if fielder is behind the base.
- If ball is **DEAD** the batter-runner is awarded first base and other runners advance only if forced by placing the batter at first base.

In any case, the runner is **NOT** declared out (while in **CONTACT** with a **BASE**) unless she **INTENTIONALLY** interferes.

Rules Reference
USSSA 8.18 N (exception), 10.3 F / NFHS 8-2 Effect 3 / ASA RS #33B, RS #44
NCAA 12.6.2

INTERFERENCE BY A RETIRED PLAYER

Interference by a runner after being called out <u>or</u> by a batter after the third strike is **INTERFERENCE** by a **RETIRED PLAYER**.

- 🔖 **NFHS:** The word "**INTENTIONALLY**" was previously **REMOVED** from the rule relating to interference by a runner who had been declared out or who had scored. **INTENT** should **NOT** be the determining factor in ruling whether interference has occurred by a runner who has scored/been retired.

- 🔖 The **BATTER is OUT** <u>and</u> the **RUNNER** closest to **HOME is OUT** regardless of which runner is being played on, if the interference prevented a double play. Other runners must return to the base last legally occupied prior to the interference.

If a **RUNNER** prevents a double-play by causing interference – the **RUNNER** is declared **OUT**, the **RUNNER** closest to **HOME** is declared out and the **BATTER** runner is **AWARDED FIRST** base. Other runners must return to the base last legally occupied prior to the interference.

All codes <u>except</u> NCAA -- Runners are never permitted to advance after an umpire rules that interference has occurred. The ball becomes dead immediately and runners (not declared out) must return to the base last legally occupied at the time of the interference. The batter-runner is not out because of interference and is awarded first base without liability to be put-out. For NCAA (see Interference on previous page 64). NCAA provides various effects whether or not the batter is IN or OUT of the batter's box. See NCAA 11.21.2 for info.

<u>Rules Reference</u>
USSSA 8.18 H / NFHS 8-2-6, 8-6-18, 5-1-1e / ASA 8-7-P / NCAA 12.19.3 (Effects)

INJURED PLAYERS

If an **INJURY** of a minor nature occurs during a **LIVE BALL** the umpire is directed to wait until:

- The **PLAY** is **COMPLETE**.
- **NO** further **PUT-OUT** is possible.
- **NO** further **ADVANCEMENT** is possible.

If the injury appears to be of a **SERIOUS NATURE** <u>or</u> the player is obviously at further **RISK** for additional injury, the umpire **MAY**:

- **STOP PLAY IMMEDIATELY** to protect an injured player.
- **NFHS / USSSA /ASA**: Umpire uses their **JUDGMENT** in determining where runners will be placed on the bases, if the ball **WAS** to have remained live.

Injured players **MAY RETURN** via the re-entry procedure if eligible.
A substitute/replacement for an injured **PITCHER** may be given ample time to warm-up prior to restarting the game. USSSA permits an injured batter / runner to be replaced by the player not currently on base who had the last completed time at bat.

*Umpires and coaches should **ALWAYS** err on the side of **CAUTION** when dealing with injured players. **USSSA / NFHS** Athletes that exhibit signs or symptoms consistent with a concussion shall be removed and not permitted to return unless cleared by an appropriate health-care professional. Return procedures also vary by state governing bodies.*

<u>Rules Reference</u>
USSSA 5.9 A / NFHS 3-3-9, 10-2-3g and k / ASA 4-10 / NCAA 15.10.2.3

JEWELRY RESTRICTIONS

USSSA/ NFHS:
Stipulate the wearing of **ANY JEWELRY** is **PROHIBITED**.

- Umpires are directed to **REMIND** players that jewelry should be removed before entering the game.
- During the pre-game conference, coaches are asked if, "**PLAYERS** are **PROPERLY EQUIPPED?**" – including the compliance with no jewelry regulations.
- 1st offense is a **TEAM WARNING** and jewelry must be **REMOVED**. 2nd offense results in the offender and head coach **RESTRICTED** to the **BENCH**.
- **ALL CODES: MEDICAL** alert bracelets may be visibly worn but must be **TAPED** to the body.
- Players will **NOT** be permitted to participate if directed and fail to remove jewelry.

ASA : Requires that exposed jewelry ruled **DANGEROUS** by the **UMPIRE** must be **REMOVED**.

USSSA / NFHS: Permit the use of hair control devices (even hard items like barrettes, bobby pins, hair clips) provided they are unadorned and no longer than 2 inches in length.

NCAA: Not regulated by umpires.

Rules Reference
USSSA 2.5; 11.2 D / NFHS 3-2-5, 3-2-12 / ASA 3-6F / NCAA (NR)

LINE- UP CARDS

REQUIREMENTS on LINE-UP CARD				
	NFHS	**ASA**	**USSSA**	**NCAA**
Line Up Cards Must Contain Starters / Available Subs	*Line Up Cards Should be Accurate - However Additional Eligible Substitures May be Added at Any Time (penalty MAY apply)*			*Eligible Subs Not Listed are Illegal Players*
Incorrect Numbers can be Corrected	*Penalized if Corrected*	*Correct with No Penalty*		*Before Card Becomes Official*
DP (Designated Player) and FLEX (Player) if Used Must Be Listed	*DP/ FLEX is Permitted*			
AP (Additional Players) if Used Must Be Listed			*1 or 2 AP's May be Used*	
Can Add Players to Lineup at Anytime	*Can Add with Penalty*	*OK to Add Eligible Players at Anytime*		*Considered Illegal Players*
First Name Required	*First Initial*	√	√	√
Last Name Required	√	√	√	√
First and Last Name	*Suggested*	√	√	√
Uniform Number and Fielding Position	*Required by All Codes*			
When is Lineup Official	*Exchanged - Verified and Accepted by Umpire*	*Inspected and Approved by Umpire*		*Reviewed and Submitted to Umpire*
May Begin with 8 Players	No	Yes		No
Game Forfeited with Number of Players	7	7	*2 Empty Batting Slots*	*Anything Less than 9*
Players in Dugout to Start Game	*Not Mentioned*	*Must be in Dugout to Start/Continue Game*		*Starters in Uniform and Dugout*

Rules Reference
USSSA 5.1 B; 5.3&4 / NFHS 3-1-3 / ASA 1-2; 4-1A; 7-2a to f
NCAA 5.6; 8.3.2

LOOK-BACK RESTRICTIONS (CIRCLE RULE)

Look-Back restrictions apply to all base runners even though the pitcher is **NOT** *actually "looking" at the runner.*

Restrictions are in **EFFECT** while:

- 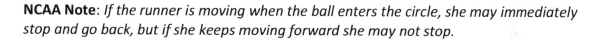 The **BALL** is **LIVE**.
- Batter-Runner has **REACHED** first base or has been declared **OUT**.
- **PITCHER** has **POSSESSION** of the ball with **BOTH** feet (completely or partially) within the **PITCHER'S CIRCLE**.
  (**ASA**: Must be in glove or hand)

RUNNERS may **STOP ONCE** then must:

- **IMMEDIATELY RETURN** to that **BASE**
                    OR
- **ATTEMPT** to **ADVANCE** to the **NEXT BASE**.

NCAA Note: *If the runner is moving when the ball enters the circle, she may immediately stop and go back, but if she keeps moving forward she may not stop.*

Once a **RUNNER STOPS** at any **BASE** then **LEAVES** that base
(while the look-back restrictions are in effect):
- She is declared **OUT.**
- The **BALL** is **DEAD**.

If the **PITCHER** in control of the ball initiates **ACTION** to cause a **REACTION** (of the runner), attempts to **MAKE-A-PLAY** on the **RUNNER**, or **LOSES CONTROL** of the ball, the runner may choose to:
- **RETURN or ADVANCE**.
- Is **NOT** restricted by the look-back restrictions.

Rules Reference
USSSA 8.2 / NFHS 8-7 / ASA 8-7t; RS #34 / NCAA 12.21

OBSTRUCTION BY THE CATCHER

Obstruction is ruled when the catcher
(or another defensive player) hinders or prevents
the **BATTER** from **HITTING** the ball.

This is a **DELAYED DEAD-BALL** play and the umpire will
signal appropriately.

OBSTRUCTION is **CANCELED** if the **BATTER**:
- **HITS** the **BALL / REACHES BASE SAFELY**.
- **ALL** other **RUNNERS** advance at least **ONE BASE**.
- **ALL ACTION** will stand – **NO OPTION**.

Otherwise the **TEAM** at bat has an **OPTION**:
- May **TAKE** the **RESULT** of the **PLAY**.
  OR
- Have **OBSTRUCTION ENFORCED** with **BATTER** awarded 1st base and
  RUNNERS ADVANCED only if **FORCED**.

If **OBSTRUCTION** occurs during an attempted steal of **HOME** plate:
- The **BATTER** is awarded 1st base.
  AND
- **USSSA / NFHS/ ASA**: Stealing/Squeeze Runner is **AWARDED HOME** if
  attempting to advance from 3rd base while other runners **ADVANCE ONLY**
  if **FORCED**.
- **NCAA: ALL RUNNERS ADVANCE** whether forced or not.

__Rules Reference__
USSSA 8.5.C & E (Notes) / NFHS 8-1-1d,e; 8-4-3b
ASA 8-1-D; 8-5B; RS #36 / NCAA 9.5.1

OBSTRUCTION BY A FIELDER

Obstruction occurs when a **FIELDER** (**NOT** in **POSSESSION** of the ball and **NOT** making an initial play) **IMPEDES** the progress of a **RUNNER** (or Batter-Runner) that is legally running the bases. Obstruction can be **PHYSICAL** or **VERBAL****.

NCAA Note: *Fielders "in the act of catching a thrown ball" are considered **NOT** to be **OBSTRUCTING** the runner.*

The **UMPIRE** should utilize the appropriate **DELAY-DEAD BALL** signal after obstruction occurs.

- **RUNNERS** are protected to the base they **WOULD** have reached, if there was **NO** obstruction.
- **RUNNERS** cannot be called out between the **TWO BASES** they were obstructed between.
- If the **OBSTRUCTED** runner(s) is tagged **OUT**, the umpire shall declare a **DEAD BALL** and award the runner(s) the base(s) they would have reached if there was **NO** obstruction.
- The ball **ALWAYS** remains **LIVE** during **OBSTRUCTION** until the umpire declares the **BALL** dead, if necessary. If the runner(s) reach their base(s) they would have reached **WITHOUT** obstruction, the umpire will drop the delay signal and the ball remains **LIVE**.

RUNNERS are not protected during **APPEAL** if **OBSTRUCTED** when **RETURNING** to touch a missed base, or base left too early on a caught fly ball.

NCAA Note: Obstructing a runner rounding or returning to a base results in an initial player warning and subsequent violations by the same individual will result in a one-base award to the obstructed runner and other runners advance if forced. (See NCAA 9.5.2.6 through 9.5.2.9)

Once a runner **OBTAINS** the base they would have reached if no obstruction occurred, and there is a **SUBSEQUENT PLAY**, they are **NO LONGER** protected if she leaves that base.

For **USSSA** and **NFHS**, **FAKE TAGS** are **ALWAYS** considered obstruction. In **ASA** and **NCAA** a fake tag must **IMPEDE** the runner to be considered obstruction.

**ASA does not mention verbal obstruction.

Rules Reference
USSSA 8.13; 11.2A / NFHS 2-21; 2-36; 8-4-3B / ASA 8-5B / NCAA 9.5.2

ON-DECK BATTER / CIRCLE

ON-DECK REQUIREMENTS	USSSA	NFHS	ASA	NCAA
Circle Size	5 Foot Diameter (2.5 Foot Radius)			
Recommended Location on Field	30 Feet from Plate Min.		Safe Distance / Location Away from Plate	
Occupant in Circle	Implied to Be Next Batter		Must be Next Batter	Any Player
Circle May Be Left Empty	Yes			Yes
Must Wear Helmet While On-Deck	At All Times in Live Ball Area and Within the On-Deck Circle			
On-Deck Batter Interferes - Effect on Runners Being Played On	Same as ASA and NCAA	Runner Played on Declared Out	**_Runner Closest to Home_** is Declared Out and Other Runners Return to Base Last Legally Occupied at the Time of Inteference	
On-Deck Batter Interferes with Fielder on Foul Fly Ball	**_Batter_** is Declared Out and Runners Must Return to Base Last Legally Occupied at the Time of Interference			
Warm Up Attachments	No Donuts or Fans - Approved Weights Permitted	Securely Attached Only	ASA Approved Devices Only	Attachments are Not Permitted in Circle
Max # of Bats in Circle	Two Bats Total Permitted			
Player Outside Bench Area	The On-Deck Batter is the Only Player Permitted to Leave the Bench Area and Be in Live Ball Territory During Play			Batter and On-Deck Batter Permitted
May Leave Circle	Only for Proper Turn at Bat, Provide Guidance to Advancing Runners from Third Base, or Avoid Interfering			
Batter During Opposing Pitcher Warm-up		Must Remain in Circle During Opposing Pitcher Warm-Up		Be in Foul Territory During Warm-Up

ASA Note: Batter may occupy either on-deck circle. Other codes, must be nearest to her dugout. All codes (except USSSA) stipulate the use of Warming Devices render the bat Altered / Illegal. USSSA permit approved models only.

Rules Reference
NFHS 1-1-6; 1-5-1a, 2-5-3 / ASA 3-5E; 3.7; 7-1; RS-16 &33D
USSSA 3.43; 1.2A; 2.11; 7.1 A; 11.2.1 / NCAA 11.1; 11.20

PITCHER'S STARTING POSITION

Pitchers may not take the **PITCHING POSITION** (**ON** or **NEAR** the pitching plate) without possession of the ball. The pitcher is not considered to be in the pitching position until the **CATCHER** is in position and ready to receive the pitch.

BODY POSITION

	USSSA	NFHS	ASA	NCAA
Pivot Foot Starting Location	*Must be On (or Partially On Top) the Pitcher's Plate*			
Non-Pivot Foot Starting Location	*In Contact with Pitcher's Plate Only*	*In Contact OR BEHIND Pitcher's Plate*	*In Contact with Pitcher's Plate Only*	
24" Width of Pitcher's Plate	*Both Feet must START and Stride Foot must FINISH within the Confines of the 24" Pitcher's Plate**			
Shoulder Positioning	*Must be In-Line with 1st and 3rd Bases to Start*			*No Requirement*
Hand Positioning	*Must Start Separated with Ball in Glove or Pitching Hand*			
Taking Signals	*Must Pause to Take (or Simulate Taking) While on Pitching Plate*			

HAND MOVEMENT

	USSSA	NFHS	ASA	NCAA
Hands Starting Position	*Prior to the Pitch the Hands Must Start Apart. (NCAA: Also when taking or simulate taking a signal from catcher.)*			
Hands Must Be Brought Together in Front of Body	*Not More Than 10 Seconds*	*Not Less than 1 Second or More Than 10 Seconds*		*In View of Umpire for No More than 5 Seconds*
Hands Can Be in Motion	*Yes*	*No Reference*	*Yes*	
Once Hands are Brought Together	*Pitcher is permitted one step forward and simultaneous with the delivery. Any step backward must begin before hands come together.*			

NCAA rules do not refer to "feet" when pitch is thrown. If taking signals from anywhere other than pitcher's plate, they must pause (2 sec.) before bringing hands together and starting motion.
*Only STRIDE FOOT must remain within 24" pitcher's plate as pitch is thrown.

Rules Reference
USSSA 6.1 / NFHS 6-1-2; 6-1-1C; 6-4-2 / ASA 6-1; RS #40 / NCAA 10.2; 10.22

PITCHER'S FOOT PLACEMENT

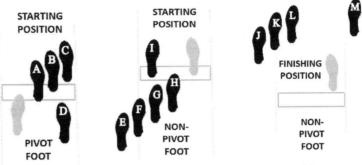

FOOT PLACEMENT (REFER to PICTURES ABOVE)				
	USSSA	NFHS	ASA	NCAA
Number of Feet Required on Plate to Start	2	1 or 2	2	2
Pivot Foot: Legal Position to Start	A or B --- Must Be in Contact (or Partial Contact) with Plate			
Pivot Foot: Illegal Position to Start	C and D --- Are Not in Contact with Plate			
Non-Pivot Foot: Legal Position to Start	H or I	F, G, H, or I	H or I	H or I
Non-Pivot Foot: Illegal Position to Start	E --- Is Not Within the 24" Length of the Pitching Plate (Lane) to Start			
Pivot Foot: Legal Position to Finish	May Be in Contact with Plate or Drag Ground in Front of Pitching Plate - Provided there is No Loss of Contact with the Ground and Replanting of Pivot Foot			
Pivot Foot: Illegal Position to Finish	Losing Contact with Ground using a Hopping Motion or Replanting of Pivot Foot During Delivery is Illegal			
Non-Pivot Foot: Legal Position to Finish	K and L --- are Legal as they are within the 24" Length of the Pitching Plate (Lane) to Finish			No reference to Non-Pivot Foot - only Stride Foot
Non-Pivot Foot: Illegal Position to Finish	J and M --- are Illegal as They Finish Outside the 24" Length of the Pitching Plate (Lane)			

Rules Reference
USSSA 6.1 / NFHS 6-1-1&2 / ASA 6-3 / NCAA 10.2-10.8

PITCH STARTS (WHEN?)

Determining when the pitch **ACTUALLY STARTS** affects the umpire's ruling for an **ILLEGAL PITCH**. Once a pitch **STARTS** it cannot be discontinued without penalty.

Terminology may be slightly different, but all codes are consistent in the ruling of when the pitch starts.

USSSA / NFHS starts when:

 **ONE HAND** is taken **OFF** the **BALL.**

<u>**OR**</u>

 When the pitcher makes **ANY KIND** of **MOTION** that is part of the **WINDUP ...**

AFTER the **HANDS** have come **TOGETHER.**

ASA / NCAA starts when:

 *the **HANDS SEPARATE** ...*

 ***AFTER** the hands have come **TOGETHER.***

*The **HANDS** may only be separated **ONE** time per pitch.*

<u>***Rules Reference***</u>
USSSA 6.1.E.1 / NFHS 6-1-2A / ASA 6-2 / NCAA 10.3

PITCHER ARM REVOLUTIONS

During the **DELIVERY** phase of the pitching motion, the following restrictions apply regarding **ARM REVOLUTIONS**:

NFHS / USSSA:
- The pitcher may **NOT** make more than 1½ **CLOCKWISE** revolutions in the windmill motion.
- The **BALL** does **NOT** have to be **RELEASED** the **FIRST** time past the **HIP**.
- After releasing the ball, the **ARM** cannot **ROTATE** past the shoulder.

ASA:
- Once the pitcher begins the **CLOCKWISE MOTION** the arm may not **MAKE 2 REVOLUTIONS**.
- May **NOT** make **ANOTHER** revolution of the pitching motion after **RELEASING** the ball.

NCAA:
- Once the pitcher begins the **CLOCKWISE MOTION** that will result in the pitch **NO MORE** than **1 ½ REVOLUTIONS**.
- May **NOT** make **ANOTHER** revolution of the pitching motion after **RELEASING** the ball.

*Effect: Violations result in an **ILLEGAL PITCH** being ruled.*

Rules Reference
USSSA 6.1.G.4 / NFHS 6-1-4D / ASA 6-3d / NCAA 10.6

PITCHER DROPS BALL

If the ball **SLIPS** from the pitcher's hand or the pitcher **DROPS** the ball **DURING DELIVERY**:

- The **BATTER** may still have the **OPPORTUNITY** to **STRIKE/SWING** at the ball.

- If batter makes a **LEGITIMATE** attempt (swinging) at the ball and **MISSES,** a **STRIKE** shall be called.

- Otherwise, it shall be ruled a **BALL** on the **BATTER**.

EFFECT:

- The **BALL** remains **LIVE**.
- **RUNNERS** may **ADVANCE** with liability to be put out.
- **DEFENSIVE PLAYERS** may **RETREIVE** the ball if **BATTER** has **NO OPPORTUNITY** to hit the ball.
- If the batter had a **REASONABLE OPPORTUNITY** to hit the ball and the defensive player retrieved it prior, this will be ruled **OBSTRUCTION**. Ball is dead and the batter and all base runners **ADVANCE** if forced. In **NCAA,** batter and runners are awarded one base whether forced or not.

Pitchers are NOT permitted to deliberately drop, roll, or bounce a ball (while in the pitching position) in order to prevent a batter from striking at the pitch. The effect is an Illegal Pitch. If a pitcher drops the ball before the pitch starts, there is no penalty. NCAA stipulates if an illegal pitch occurs but the pitch is not released, it is a dead ball.

Rules Reference
USSSA 6.1.M / NFHS 6-2-6 /ASA 6-11 / NCAA 10.7

PITCHER/BATTER TIMING

All codes provide guidelines for both pitcher and batter to keep the flow of a game moving properly. Failure to comply results in a **BALL** awarded or a **STRIKE** given to the batter.

PITCHER REQUIREMENTS	USSSA	NFHS	ASA	NCAA
Pitcher Must Comply After Receiving Ball from Catcher	*Release Pitch within* **20** *Seconds*			*10 - 10 - 5 Second Timing Provisions (SEE BELOW**)*
Failure to Comply	*Ball is Awarded to the Batter*			
BATTER REQUIREMENTS	**USSSA**	**NFHS**	**ASA**	**NCAA**
Once Ball is Returned to Pitcher or Directed by Umpire	*Take Position in the Batter's Box Within* **10** *Seconds*			
Failure to Comply	*Strike is Given to the Batter*			

**NCAA Pitchers *must comply with the following timing sequences:*

- On **PITCHER'S PLATE** within **10 SEC** after receiving ball from catcher or umpire calls, "play ball."
- After batter/pitcher are in position, pitcher has up to another **10 SEC** to **BRING** her **HANDS TOGETHER**.
- The pitcher then has up to **5 SEC** to **DELIVER** pitch.
- **VIOLATING ANY** of these timing sequences results in a **BALL** to the **BATTER**.

Since a clock is not utilized and umpires are not required to keep visible counts (like other sports) the timing restrictions should be penalized judiciously and only to prevent unnecessary delays or players from creating an unfair advantage by delaying the game.

Rules Reference
USSSA 6.1 K; 7.8 / NFHS 6-2-3; 7-3-1 / ASA 6-3o; 7-3b / NCAA 10.18; 11.2.1

PITCHER - ILLEGAL PITCH SUMMARY

PITCHER VIOLATIONS				
	USSSA	NFHS	ASA	NCAA
Pitching Plate Violations	Not Starting with Feet in Proper Position in Relation to Plate (see section on Pitcher's Starting Position)			
Pitching Lane Violations	Not Finishing with Feet (or NCAA=Stride Foot) within 24" Length of Pitcher's Plate / Lane (see section on Pitcher's Foot Placement)			
Taking Signals	Not Taking (or Simulate Taking) Catcher's Signal from Plate			
Bringing Hands Together	Failure to Bring Hands Together or Keeping Hands Together for Longer than Prescribed Time Limit			
Taking Position on Plate	Violation if Pitcher Does Not Have Ball On the Plate or Taking Position with the Ball Near the Pitcher's Plate			
Remove Pitcher from Pitching Position	Stepping Sideways or Forward is Illegal Only Stepping Backward is Legal to Remove Pitcher from Plate			
Pivot Foot Violations	Wrong Position, Leaping, or Hopping with Pivot Foot			
Arm Motion or Revolution Violations	Excessive, Improper, or Illegal Movement of the Pitching Arm (see section on Pitcher Arm Revolutions)			
Deliberately Drop, Roll, or Bounce Ball to Batter	Violation to Pitch Ball by Rolling or Bouncing Whereas the Batter Has No Ability to Strike at the Ball (see section on Pitcher Drops Ball)			
Illegal or Distracting Substance / Tape on Pitching Hand	Based on Specific Code - Certain Substances (and Tape) are Illegal (see section on Pitching Miscellaneous)			

CATCHER VIOLATIONS			
	USSSA	NFHS	ASA
Not in Proper Position for Pitch	Not in the Catcher's Box when Pitcher is in Position for Pitch		

FIELDER VIOLATIONS			
	USSSA	NFHS	ASA
Acts to Distract the Batter	Include Taking a Position in the Line of a Batter's Vision or In Foul Territory including Unsportsmanlike Acts Designed to Distract the Batter		

*For penalties ... see **ILLEGAL PITCH PENALTY** on next page.*

Rules Reference

USSSA 6.1.a through k / NFHS 6-2-1 & 3 / ASA 6-1 through 7 / NCAA 10.1

PITCHER – ILLEGAL PITCH PENALTY

If the pitch is **NOT RELEASED**
(or released to a base):

The **UMPIRE** should declare an immediate
DEAD BALL.

- Runners are directed to **ADVANCE ONE BASE** by the umpire.
- The **BATTER** is also awarded a **BALL**.

If the pitch **IS RELEASED,** the umpire shall signal **DELAY DEAD BALL** (while verbalizing- **ILLEGAL**) **AND** …

If the batter does **NOT HIT** the pitch (or become a base runner):

- The umpire should then signal **DEAD BALL.**
- The **RUNNERS** will then be directed to **ADVANCE ONE BASE** by the umpire.
- The **BATTER** is also awarded a **BALL**.

If the **RELEASED** pitch **IS HIT** by the batter or the **BATTER BECOMES** a **BASE RUNNER** the batting team can choose:

- To accept the **RESULT** of the batter's **PLAY** on the ball.
- To accept the **PENALTY** – a ball is awarded to the batter and the runner(s) advance one base.

Exception: If the **BATTER BECOMES** a **BASE RUNNER** and **ALL OTHER BASE RUNNERS** have **ADVANCED** at least **ONE BASE** – then **NO OPTION** is given.

Rules Reference
USSSA 6.1.A through K – Effect / NFHS 5-1-1p; 6-2-7; 6-1-1d
ASA 6-1 to 5, 7A, and 8 Effect A-D / NCAA 10.8

PITCHER – NO PITCH GUIDELINES

The umpire shall declare the ball dead immediately by verbalizing
NO PITCH when these situations occur:

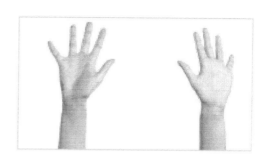

- If the pitcher delivers the ball during the time **PLAY** is **SUSPENDED** – when the umpire has declared **TIME** is **OUT.**

- The pitch is delivered before the umpire directs the pitcher to **PLAY BALL** and makes a **DEAD BALL** – live again <u>or</u> a **BATTER** steps out of the box causing a **DOUBLE VIOLATION** prior to a legal pitch.

- Pitcher tries to "**QUICK PITCH**" the ball when the batter is not given the proper **OPPORTUNITY** to take a position within the batter's box or is off balance from the previous pitch.

- After a **FOUL BALL**, the pitcher delivers a pitch to a batter **BEFORE** any runners had the opportunity to **RE-TOUCH** their previously occupied base.

- A coach or player calls **TIME** for the distinct purpose of causing the pitcher throw an illegal pitch.

- **USSSA, NFHS, ASA**: If a runner **LEAVES** a base **BEFORE** the pitcher **RELEASES** the ball from her hand and is called **OUT** – the ball is dead immediately and all subsequent action is cancelled.

- **NCAA**: A runner leaving early is considered a **Delayed Dead Ball**. At the conclusion of the play the coach of the defensive team shall have the option of (1) taking the result of the play <u>or</u> (2) "**no pitch**" is declared, the batter is returned to the batter's box and the offending runner is out. Base runners must return to the base legally occupied at the time of the pitch.

Rules Reference
USSSA 6.3 / NFHS 6-2-4c / ASA 6-10 / NCAA 10.9; 10.10

PITCHING MISCELLANEOUS

REQUIREMENT	USSSA	NFHS	ASA	NCAA
Warm Up Pitches Between Innings	Maximim of **5** Pitches Permitted ** Additional Pitches Permitted if Replacing Injured Pitcher			
Warm Up Time Between Innings	Maximim of **1** Minute Permitted Additional Time Permitted if Replacing an Injured Pitcher			Not Specified
Deliver Pitch Behind Pitcher's Back or Through Legs	Illegal by Rule			Legal
Fielder's / Catcher's Positioning	Fielders Must Be in Fair Territory and Catcher in Catcher's Box Before the Pitch is Released			
Wearing Distracting Items	Pitcher may Not Wear any Distracting Items on the Pitching Hand, Elbow, Forearm, or either Thigh.			
Tape on Pitching Hand or Fingers	Nothing Distracting	Not Permitted on Contact Points	Nothing Distracting	Neutral Color
Resin Bag / Drying Agent Permitted	Permitted to Ulitilize and Leave in the Pitcher's Circle. Gorilla Gold tacky agent is approved for USSSA,			

** NCAA will permit up to one throw to first base as part of the five pitch warm-up. USSSA stipulates no tacky or sticky substances can be used as a substitute for a powdered drying agent.

 Umpires will typically remind the pitcher/catcher they are not to exceed 5 pitches between innings – and if they choose to take a warm-up throw down to second base, it should be no later than after the 5th warm-up pitch. Umpires may elect to advise the pitcher/catcher the warm-up period is over if the time limit of one minute has been exceeded due to the defensive team being delayed in taking the field to start the inning.

Rules Reference
USSSA 6.1 / NFHS 6-2-2,5&9; 6-1-3C /ASA 6-9; 6-3F; 6-5A; 6-6B / NCAA 10.19, 10.13

RETURNING to a MISSED BASE

When a runner **MISSES** a **BASE** or **LEAVES** a base **TOO SOON**, there are restrictions on how and when the runner must re-touch the base to avoid being called out on appeal.

ABILITY to RETURN				
	USSSA	NFHS	ASA	NCAA
Ball Remains Live	*Runners **MAY** Return to Touch a Missed Base - In Reverse Order without Skipping Any Bases While Returning to the Missed Base*			
Before Defensive Team Performs Appeal (Implied Live Ball)				
Standing on a Base Beyond the One Missed **	*After This Timeframe --- Runners are **NOT** Permitted to Return and Touch Missed Bases*			
Once the Ball Becomes Dead				
Once Time is Called				
Once Following Runner Scored				
Once a Runner Leaves the Field of Play or Enters Bench Area				
Once a Runner Touches the FINAL BASE of a Dead Ball Award				
Returning to Touch Missed Bases	*Missed Bases Must be Touched in Reverse Order Runner May Not Skip Bases and Go Directly to the Base Missed*			
Touching Awarded Bases	*Awarded Bases Must be Touched in Order*			
Ball Thrown Into Dead Ball Area While Runner is Attempting to Return	*Even though the Ball is Dead - the Returning Runner Should be Given the Opportunity to Re-Touch Missed Bases (or Ones Left Early) if She is Attempting to Return*			

** And Time is Called by the Umpire

Rules Reference
USSSA 8.6.c,h&i; 9.6 / NFHS 8-3; 8-4-3h; 2-1-3a / ASA 8-3G; 8-5G; RS#1D
NCAA 7.1.4; 12.8.3; 12.10; 12.22

RUNNER RESTRICTIONS

ALL CODES: RUNNERS attempting to advance **MAY** legally do the following:

Move **FORWARD** and **BACKWARD** between the bases – **UNLESS**:

A **PLAY** is being made on the **RUNNER** – then they must stay within a **3-FOOT BASE PATH** (in a **STRAIGHT LINE**) from their **CURRENT POSITION** to the base when trying to **AVOID** a **FIELDER** in possession of the **BALL**.

MOVING BACKWARD EXCEPTION (ALL CODES):
The **BATTER-RUNNER** advancing from the **BATTER'S BOX** toward **1st base** –
is restricted from moving **BACKWARD** to avoid a **TAG**. **EFFECT**: The Batter-Runner is declared **OUT** and runners return to the last base occupied at the time of infraction (or NCAA, time of pitch).

Runners **MAY HURDLE** or **JUMP** another player provided:

- **ASA / NCAA**: The **RUNNER** is trying to **AVOID** a **TAG** and the defender is **HOLDING** the **BALL**.

- **USSSA / NFHS**: The **FIELDER** is **OFF** their **FEET** and **LYING ON** the **GROUND**. However, if the fielder is **STANDING**, **STOOPING**, or **CROUCHED** the runner may **NOT LEAP** over them.

*Note: The Standard Effect for this violation is **INTERFERENCE**.*

Rules Reference
USSSA 8.18.A and C (Note) / NFHS 8-6-1&10 / ASA 8-8
NCAA 12.4; 12.19.6 Note

RUNNERS SWITCHING BASES

If runners **SWITCH** bases after a dead ball <u>or</u> charged conference the following will apply:

EFFECT	NFHS	ASA	USSSA	NCAA
Specific Rule Coverage	Yes			Yes
Effect on Runners	Each Runner on Improper Base is Out		No Reference	Each Runner on Improper Base is Out
The Offending Head Coach is Ejected	May be Ruled Unsportsmanlike Conduct if Intentionally Done by Coach / Manager			Head Coach Ejected
Player Removal	Restricted to Bench if Deliberate			Players Involved are Ejected
Can Be Enforced	Not an Appeal Play -- Can Be Enforced Anytime Detected by the Umpire			Appeal Play After Ball is Put Back into Play

Intentionally switching players on base during a dead ball is considered unsportsmanlike and should be penalized accordingly. Though not specifically covered in USSSA rules, it may be penalized as such.

Rules Reference
USSSA 11.2.R / NFHS 8-6-4; 10-2-3f / ASA 8-7Y / NCAA 12.5.3

SPECTATOR INTERFERENCE

When a spectator reaches into the field of play and **INTERFERES** with a **LIVE BALL** the following is in effect:

ALL CODES: The **BALL** is **DEAD** once a spectator **TOUCHES** the live ball in play.

USSA / NFHS / NCAA:

⚾ The **UMPIRE** should award the offended team the **PROPER** compensation (or result) that would have occurred if interference would **NOT** have happened.

NCAA Note: *If Spectator Interference clearly prevented a fielder from catching a fly ball in the field of play, the ball is dead, the batter is out, and the umpire shall award the appropriate compensation (for example, return base runners to bases, an out, or advance a runner) that, in his or her opinion, would have resulted had interference not taken place.*

ASA :

⚾ If the **SPECTATOR** interfered with a fielder's ability to catch a **FLY BALL**, the **BATTER** is **OUT** and **RUNNERS** are **AWARDED** (or **RETURNED** to) the bases they would have reached if there was **NO** interference.

Rules Reference
USSSA 8.14.E / NFHS 8-4-3k / ASA 8-2N / NCAA 4.9, 12.12.6.2, 12.19

STRIKE ZONE (DEFINED)

USSSA – NFHS- ASA

A **STRIKE** shall be called if **ANY PART** of the **BALL** (without touching the ground) passes through:

The **SPACE** over **HOME PLATE** <u>AND</u>:

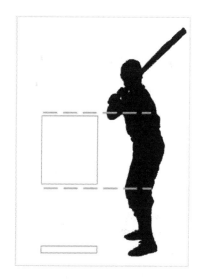

- **BETWEEN** the batter's **FORWARD ARMPIT** and the top of the **KNEES**.

- If the batter assumes a **NATURAL** stance.
  (See diagram to the right)

NCAA

A **STRIKE** shall be called if **TOP** and/or **SIDES** of the **BALL** passes through:

The **SPACE** over **HOME PLATE** <u>AND</u>:

- The **BOTTOM** of the batter's **STERNUM** and to the top of the **KNEES**.
- If the batter assumes a **NATURAL** batting stance.
- The **TOP** of the ball must be on or within the **HORIZONTAL PLANE**, and either **SIDE** of the ball must be on or within the **VERTICAL PLANE** of the strike zone to be a strike unless the ball touches the ground before reaching home plate.

(See updated / clarified NCAA Strike Zone Diagram in the 2016-17 NCAA Rule Book)

When determining the boundaries of a batter's strike zone, the umpire is directed to take notice of the player's "natural stance" within the batter's box. Pitchers should not be penalized for players that crouch down excessively to minimize the strike zone area and intentionally try to draw a walk.

Rules Reference
USSSA 3.57 / NFHS 2-56-3 / ASA 1 / NCAA 11.3.1

SUBSTITUTIONS (LEGAL)

REQUIREMENTS	USSSA	NFHS	ASA	NCAA
Re-Entry Permitted	All Starters and Substitutes Permitted to Re-Enter One Time			Starters ONLY One Time
Substitute Officially In Game When Reported to Plate Umpire	When Reported	And Ball Becomes Live	When Reported	When Reported, Recorded, and Announced
Minimum to Start Game	8 Players	9 Players	8 Players	9 Players
Minimum Number of Players to Finish	1 Less than Started With	8 Players to Continue or Complete Game		9 Players
Effect When Reaching Absent Player	Out is Declared			Not Applicable
If No Available Substitutes to Replace Injured Player	See Note Below*	Previous Batter May Replace		Forfeit
Player Arrives Late or Injured Player Wishes to Return	Player Arriving Late May be Inserted into Missing Player Line-up Spot -- Injured Players Must Re-Enter into the Same Line-up Spot as Prior			Considered Illegal Player if Not on Lineup Card
Blood Rule	Players Leaving the Game to Address Blood on Body or Blood on Uniform are Permitted to Return			May be Treated without Undue Delay or Penalty
Team Can Walk or Accidently Hit Batter to Reach Absent Player	Permitted	No Reference	Permitted	Not Applicable

USSSA Note: Courtesy runner may be used in same ½ inning she was C.R. or she may be replaced by last batter not on base. The injured player may not return.

Rules Reference
USSSA 5.2; 5.6; 5.8; 7.14E, 8.3D / NFHS 3-3-3; 3-1-1; 3-3-8; 4-3-1g; 3-3-5
ASA 4-6b; 4-1d; 4-5/ NSA 4.3; 4-4-b&c / NCAA 8.5

SUBSTITUTIONS (UNREPORTED)

When a **PLAYER** participates in the game **WITHOUT** **REPORTING** to the **UMPIRE** the following will apply:

EFFECT				
	USSSA	NFHS	ASA	NCAA
How UnReported Subs are Handled	*Umpire Can Take Action when Noticed or Brought to Their Attention*		*By Protest*	*By Appeal*
After Next Pitch (Legal/Illegal) the Play Stands	*After Team Warning Becomes Legal Player*	*Yes*	*Except Batter Reaches 1st Base*	*Player is Called Out and In Game*
No Penalty if the Violating Team				*Informs Plate Umpire before Offended Team's Challenge*
1st Offense Results In (Effect)	*Team Warning*	*Head Coach Warning*	*If Before Next Pitch - Player is OUT - Runners Return*	*Depending on timing ... results in Player Called OUT and varying effects on the Resulting Play (See NCAA Rules)*
Next Offense Results In (Effect)	*Coach Ejection*	*Offender AND Coach Restricted to Bench*		

Rules Reference
USSSA 5.5 / NFHS 3-6-7 / ASA 4-6C / NCAA 8.3.3

SUBSTITUTIONS (ILLEGAL) DEFINED

A player that **ENTERS** (or **RE-ENTERS**) the game and does **NOT** have **ELIGIBILITY** or is **NOT ENTITLED** to enter is considered illegal.

Examples include:

- **RE-ENTERING** in the **WRONG** position in the **BATTING ORDER**.
- **FLEX** player violations -- such as entering the lineup in a spot **OTHER THAN** the **DESIGNATED PLAYER (DP)** spot.
- **COURTESY-RUNNER** violations.
- **RE-ENTERING** the game after being disqualified or ejected.
- **ILLEGAL** pitcher, batter, or runner.

Players become an **ILLEGAL** substitute:

- **NFHS**: When ball becomes **LIVE** and player **TAKES POSITION** (in batter's box, on pitcher's plate, in field, or on base).
- **ASA / USSSA**: Once entering the game (at bat/position) and one pitch is thrown.
- **NCAA**: When the plate umpire **RECORDS** the substitution **or** she **COMPETES** in the game. Handled as an **APPEAL**.

ASA:	Ejected participants discovered in the game are grounds for **FORFEIT**.
USSSA/ASA:	Does not consider the wrong **TIE-BREAKER** runner as illegal.
NCAA:	**NON-STARTER** re-entering, player **NOT LISTED** on the line-up card, wrong **TIE-BREAKER** runner, is considered an illegal player.
NFHS:	Refers to Illegal Substitutes as Illegal **PLAYERS**.

Rules Reference
USSSA 5.7 / NFHS 3-4 / ASA 4-6 / NCAA 8.3.4, Appendix B

SUBSTITUTIONS (ILLEGAL) EFFECT

ILLEGAL PLAYERS are **REMOVED** from the game when discovered. The delivery of the **NEXT PITCH** does **NOT LEGALIZE** an **ILLEGAL PLAYER** – she still is **REMOVED.** Depending on **WHEN** this is detected (in relation to the **NEXT PITCH** to the **NEXT BATTER**) determines the specific **EFFECT** based on various codes

– see next page.

Applies to NFHS <u>PRIOR</u> to NEXT PITCH:

Can be discovered by **EITHER TEAM** or **UMPIRE** once the ball becomes **LIVE** and the illegal player takes a position in the **BATTER'S BOX,** in the **FIELD,** or replaces player as a **SUBSTITUTE** or **COURTESY RUNNER.**

The **PLAYER** is **RESTRICTED** to the **BENCH** for the remainder of the game and called **OUT** if on **OFFENSE**.

If offender advances, scored or causes other players to advance/score the **PLAY** is **NULLIFIED** and runners must **RETURN** to base occupied at the time of pitch.

If illegal **DEFENDER** touches a batted ball or handles a thrown ball that leads to a runner being put-out (or alters play) – additionally the **OFFENSE** may elect to take the results of the play or accept the penalty (nullify play). Umpire **MAY** award bases based on their judgment.

Batter is permitted to **BAT AGAIN** with the same count (if batted ball) or pitch is cancelled if a strike (for a thrown ball.)

Once the **NEXT PITCH** is thrown to the following batter (for either team) the **PLAY STANDS** however the **ILLEGAL PLAYER** is **REMOVED**.

<u>*Rules Reference*</u>
USSSA 5.7 / NFHS 3-4 / ASA 4-6 / NCAA 8.3.4, Appendix B
(See Other Codes on Next Page)

SUBSTITUTIONS (ILLEGAL) EFFECT

SITUATION / EFFECT				
	USSSA	NFHS	ASA	NCAA
Offending Team Corrects Own Mistake (Offense or Defense)	*Action Before a Pitch is Thrown or Play Made Can be Corrected if Not Appealed*	*No Penalty if Prior to Ball Becoming Live*	*Player is DQ'd and All Play Stands*	*Offending Player is Ejected and All Play Stands*
Defense Team Alerts Umpire (Offender is At-Bat*)	*Player and Coach are Ejected and Player is Called Out*	*Player is Called Out and Restricted to Bench*	*Player is DQ'd and All Play Stands if Protested*	*Offending Player is Out and Ejected - Nullify Advances on Last Pitch but All Previous Advances are Legal*
Defense Team Alerts Umpire (After At-Bat or Courtesy Runner) PRIOR to Next PITCH)	*Player and Coach are Ejected Player is Called Out Advance is Nullified and Outs Stand*	*Player is Called Out and Restricted to Bench - Advance is Nullified and Outs Stand*	*Player is Called Out and DQ'd -- Nullify Advances and Outs Stand*	
Defense Team Alerts Umpire (After At-Bat or Courtesy Runner) AFTER Next PITCH)	*Player and Coach are Ejected -- All Play Stands*	*Player is Restricted to Bench - All Play Stands*	*Player is DQ'd -- Sub Enters -- All Play Stands*	*Offending Player is Out and Ejected - All Advances Are Legal*
Offensive Team Alerts Umpire (After Defensive Player Makes Play - PRIOR to Next PITCH)	*Player and Coach Ejected -- Offended Team's Option to Take Play Results OR Replaying Last Pitch*	*Player Restricted to Bench -- Offended Team's Option to Take Play Results OR Nullify Play-- Umpire May Award Bases*	*Player is DQ'd-- Offended Coach has Option to Take Play Results or Return to Bat with Same Count and Runners Return*	*Offensive Coach has Option to Nullify Play and Repeat Last Pitch - OR - Take the Results of the Play and Offending Player is Ejected*
Offensive Team Alerts Umpire (After Defensive Player Makes Play - AFTER Next PITCH)	*Player and Coach are Ejected All Play Stands*	*Player Restricted to Bench -- All Play Stands*	*Player is DQ'd and All Play Stands*	*All Play Stands AND the Offending Player is Ejected*

(Rule References on Previous Page)

UNIFORMS

SPECIFICATIONS	USSSA	NFHS	ASA	NCAA
Same Color and Style	All Team Members Shall be Alike - Style, Color, and Trim			
Pants / Shorts	. Must ALL Wear either Pants or Shorts - Not Mixed		May Mix but Same Color	Same as USSSA/ NFHS
Minimum Number Size	3"	6"		
Opposing Team Uniform Colors	No Mention on Specific Color			Visiting Team is Required to Wear Contrasting Color
Manufacturer's Logo	No Reference	2¼ " Max.	No Other Assoc. Permitted	2¼ " Max.
Caps, Visors, and Headbands	Must be Same Type	Mixed Types -Same Color Bandanas Not Permitted. ASA does not consider headbands part of uniform, and not regulated.		Visors / Hats may be Mixed but Same Color - Headbands Not Regulated
Sleeves		Approx. Same Length	Not Ragged	Same Solid Color - Style and Length May Vary
Exposed Undergarments (Team Color or ..)	If Worn Same Color by All Players	White, Black or Grey - All Players Same	Same Color by All Players	Solid School Color OR Black, White, or Gray with All Same Color
Jewelry	Remove	Not Permitted	Remove Dangerous	Not Regulated
Metal Cleats	13U and Above	Permitted by State	Permitted	
Casts and Splints	Padded - Not Pose a Threat for Injury to Another Athlete			
Blood	Change Uniform No Penalty	Uniform Cleaned or Changed	Change Uniform No Penalty	
Penalty for Uniform Violation	Remove		Remove or No Play	Remove

NCAA (New 2016-17): Plastic Visors, Bandanas, and Hankerchiefs are now permissible.

Rules Reference
USSSA 2.4A, 2.8 / NFHS 3-2&3 / ASA 3-6 / NCAA 3.10

DROPPED THIRD STRIKE

The Rule. The Amateur Softball Association defines the **dropped third strike rule** in **Rule 8,** Section 1B: "When the catcher fails to catch the **third strike** before the ball touches the ground and there are fewer than two outs and first base is not occupied at the time of the pitch <u>or</u> any time there ar **two outs."** Sep 11, 2017

INDEX to REFERENCES

A

ALTERED BATS...27
APPEALS
    How they are made...................................22
    Miscellaneous...23
    Types of Appeals 21
APPEALS – ALL TYPES.....................................21
Appeals, more than one. 23

B

BALL LODGES in UNIFORM 24
BALL ROTATION PROCEDURE
    Pitcher Choice of Balls to Start Inning 25
    Pitcher Compares Balls Side to Side 25
    Pitcher requests new ball..........................25
BAT – LEGAL / ILLEGAL
    Approved Bat List 26
    Banned Bat List 26
    Certification Marks..................................26
    Effect..27
    Requirements 26
    Use of Illegal Bat....................................27
Bats
    Certification Marks..................................26
    General Requirements 26
    Grip and Knob...26
    Grip Length 26
    Knobs 26
    Maximum Length 26
    Maximum Weight 26
    Tacky Substances....................................26
BATTER / PITCHER TIMING 84
BATTER HITS BALL TWICE 28
BATTER POSITIONING.....................................31
BATTER PREVENTS BALL from 29
BATTER STEPS OUT of the BOX.......................30
BATTER STRUCK by PITCH...............................32
BATTER-RUNNER OVERRUNS FIRST 33
BATTER-RUNNER STEPS BACKWARD 34
BATTING - OUT of ORDER 35
Billy Martin Bio..3
BLOCKED BALL
    Defined 37
    Effect..38
BUNT ATTEMPT...39

C

CATCH – DEFINED...40
CATCH and CARRY 41
CATCHER RETURNS BALL to PITCHER 42
Cell phones..57
CHARGED CONFERENCE (DEFENSE)................45
CHARGED CONFERENCE (OFFENSE)................44
CHARGED CONFERENCES 43
CHECKED SWING 46
COLLAPSIBLE FENCES......................................47
CONTRIBUTORS 5
COURTESY RUNNERS 48

D

Dead Ball Appeal 21
DOUBLE BASES..50
DP / FLEX GUIDELINES.....................................52

E

EJECTIONS- Where do they go? 56
ELECTRONIC EQUIPMENT 57
EQUIPMENT VERIFICATION and MISUSE.........59
ERASING CHALK LINES.....................................58

F

Forfeit - Who Declares?....................................60
FORFEIT SITUATIONS.......................................60
Forfeits and Game Termination 61

G

GAME LIMITS 61
GLOVE ILLEGAL USE 63
GLOVE REQUIREMENTS...................................62
    Colors...62
    Height 62
    Webbing 62
    Width 62

H

Helmet Requirements
- Base Coaches on Field 64
- Catcher Eye Shields 64
- Chin Strap..64
- Face Guards 64
- Intentionally Removing Helmet 64
- NOCSAE Seal 64

HELMET REQUIREMENTS...64

HITS BALL TWICE 28

Hurdling Another Player 90

I

ILLEGAL PITCH PENALTY...86

Illegal Pitch Summary 85
- Pitching Lane Violations 85
- Pitching Plate Violations..85

Implied Appeal 22

Improper Batter...35

INJURED PLAYERS..72

Interference by a Retired Player 71

INTERFERENCE by the BATTER.................................66

INTERFERENCE by the RUNNER 68

INTERFERENCE DEFINED 65

INTERFERENCE: BALL TOUCHES RUNNER on BASE 70

J

JEWELRY RESTRICTIONS..73

L

LINE- UP CARDS..74

Live Ball Appeal 21

LOOK-BACK RESTRICTIONS 75

M

Malicious Contact 65

Metal Cleats 99

Missing Home Plate Appeal.......................................23

O

OBSTRUCTION by a FIELDER 77

OBSTRUCTION by the CATCHER 76

ON-DECK BATTER / CIRCLE
- Interference..78
- Location 78
- Number of Bats 78
- Occupants..78
- Size 78
- Warm-Up Attachments....................................78
- Wearing of Helmet..78

P

PITCH STARTS..81

PITCHER – ILLEGAL PITCH PENALTY 86

PITCHER – NO PITCH GUIDELINES 87

PITCHER ARM REVOLUTIONS 82

PITCHER DROPS BALL 83

PITCHER/BATTER TIMING...84

PITCHER'S FOOT PLACEMENT
- Non-Pivot Foot 80
- Pivot Foot 80

PITCHER'S STARTING POSITION
- Body Position...79
- Hand Position 79

PITCHING MISCELLANEOUS...88
- Distracting Items 88
- Resin Bag 88
- Tape on Pitching Hand 88
- Warm Up Pitches 88
- Warm Up Time Between Innings.........................88

Pre-Game Conference...59

Proper Batter 35

R

REFERENCES 7
RETURNING to a MISSED BASE 89
Rule Changes
    NFHS 10
RULE CHANGES
    ASA 12
    NCAA 14
    USSSA 13
RUNNER RESTRICTIONS 90
Runner Vacating Base 70
RUNNERS SWITCHING BASES 91

S

SPECTATOR INTERFERENCE 92
STRIKE ZONE (DEFINED) 93
SUBSTITUTIONS (ILLEGAL) DEFINED 96
SUBSTITUTIONS (ILLEGAL) EFFECT 97
SUBSTITUTIONS (LEGAL) 94
SUBSTITUTIONS (UNREPORTED) 95

T

Team(s) Fail to Appear 60
Team(s) Refuse to Begin / Continue 60
Tim Malloy Bio 4
TOUCHING a MISSED BASE 23

U

UNIFORM, LODGED BALL 24
UNIFORMS 99
    Caps, Visors, Headbands 99
    Color and Style 99
    Exposed Undergarments 99
    Jewelry 99
    Logo 99
    Metal Cleats 99
    Minimum Number Size 99
    Sleeves 99

For updates to this reference please visit:

bluebook60.com

Attention: HS / College Basketball Officials

"Beyond the Rules - Volumes 1 & 2" plus the *"Best of 60 Seconds on Officiating"* is available on Amazon. Visit the following website:

gobeyondtherules.com

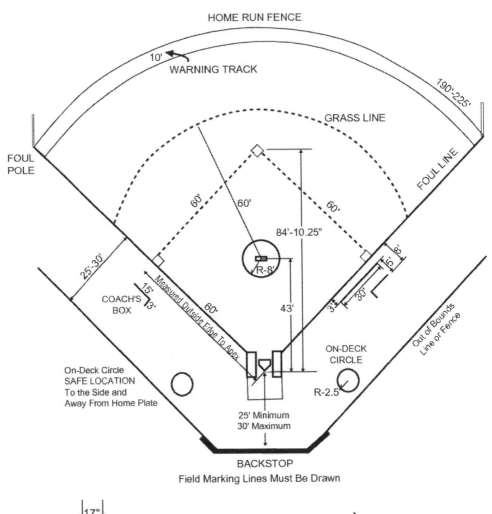

HOME RUN FENCE

WARNING TRACK

10'

GRASS LINE

190'-225'

FOUL POLE

FOUL LINE

60'   60'   60'

84'-10.25"

R-8'

25'-30'

Measured Outside Edge To Apex

COACH'S BOX

15'   3'

60'

15'   8'

3'   30'

43'

Out of Bounds Line or Fence

On-Deck Circle SAFE LOCATION To the Side and Away From Home Plate

ON-DECK CIRCLE

R-2.5

25' Minimum 30' Maximum

BACKSTOP

Field Marking Lines Must Be Drawn

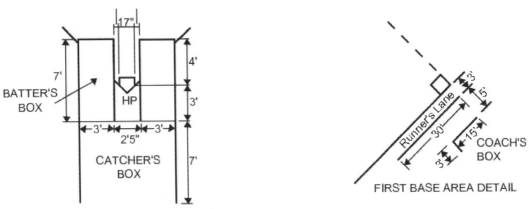

17"

4'

7'

BATTER'S BOX

HP

3'

3'   3'

2'5"

7'

CATCHER'S BOX

Runner's Lane

3'

5'

30'

3'

15'

COACH'S BOX

FIRST BASE AREA DETAIL

Appendix: Umpire Resources

An NCAA protests is a "formal inquiry" into the decision of an umpire and is only permitted (by NCAA) in the following situations:

- Failure to apply the correct RULE in a situation.
- Failure to impose the correct effect for a given violation of the rules.
- Misapplication of a playing rule.

They will **NOT** be received (or considered) if they are based solely on the accuracy of judgement of an umpire.

Protests may involve matters of both judgement <u>and</u> the misinterpretation of a rule but not judgement solely.

NCAA protest procedure should be carried out by the umpire crew on the field using the checklist provided.

Cut, fold and laminate this for easy reference in your ball bag. See NCAA Rule 7.2 for more information.

NCAA Protest Checklist

- ❑ Before Next Pitch (Legal or Illegal)
- ❑ Before Umpires Leave Field
- ❑ Umpire Decision Violates Rule (not Judgement or Application of Effect)
- ❑ Coach ID's Actual Rule Violated
- ❑ Opponent Coach May Input
- ❑ Use Rule Book – Timely Fashion
- ❑ Crew Privately Meets / Discuss
- ❑ 1st Attempt to Settle
- ❑ Bring Both Coaches Together – Explain Ruling – Use Rule Book
- ❑ Last Chance to Settle
- ❑ Call NCAA Rules Secretary for On-Field Resolution
  #(   ) _____

- ❑ Continue Under Protest
- ❑ PU announces to Opposing Coach, Scorer, PA – Game is Continuing Under Protest
- ❑ PU records opponent, date, time, place, crew names, scorer name, rule / section protested, essential facts and contact info.
- ❑ Protesting Team Wins = No Protest
- ❑ Protesting Team Loses = PU notifies NCAA Rules Secretary post game
- ❑ 24 Hours = PU + Both Coaches File NCAA Incident Report

Fastpitch Pregame Discussion Points – 2 Person Crews

Basic Umpire Responsibilities

PU
- Batted Balls
- Fair/Foul
- Catch/No Catch
- Plays at Plate / When Cover 3B?
- Illegal Pitch – Lane / Hands
- Batter-Runner Tag Plays Halfway

BU
- Runners Touch
- All Plays at 1st and 2nd
- Batter-Runner @ 3rd
- Initial Play from IF @ 3rd
- Illegal Pitch - Feet

Special Rules
- Tie breaker? Inning?
- Run Rule?

Fly Ball Coverage / Chase
- PU unless BU Chases
- BU Chase Situations:
  - 1B Line in A Position
  - Troubled Fly Balls

BU
- BU (B / C Pos.) – Chase the V
- Make OF Come Toward You
- BU No Return After Chase
- BU Turn and Observe

Tag-Up Responsibilities

PU
- All Tags at 3rd
- Lead Runner with
  Multiple Runners On-Base
- All Tags if BU Chases

BU
- All Tags at 1st
- All Trail Runner(s) Tagging
- (NCAA) BU Tag @ 2nd and
  PU takes Runner into 3rd
- No Tags if Chasing

Leaving Base Early

BU
- Dead ball (NFHS / ASA / USSSA)
- Delayed Dead Ball (NCAA)
- Options – (Discuss / Present)
  With no defensive violation
  With defensive violation

Checked Swings

PU
- Procedure
- Asked by Catcher
- Asked by Others

Pickoff Coverage

BU
- Runner @ 1st – BU in C-Position?
  Be Ready to Help (if asked)

Umpire to Umpire Signals

PU **BU**
- Dropped/Caught 3rd strike
- Infield fly On/Off
- Two Out / Timing Play
- Request # of Outs?
- Request the Count
- Between Inning Positions

PU **BU** Two Person Crew -- Special Situations

Help from Partner

-Checked Swing (Catcher)

-Pickoff Attempts

-Missing Piece of Puzzle

-Procedure

Crew Confer Alone

Calling Umpire Give Decision

Confrontations / Ejections

-Discuss Play Made Only

-Make Coach Ask Question

-Partner Intervene as Needed

-Proper Escort Procedure

Leaving the Field of Play

-Know the Route Before Start

-Crew Leaves Together

-No Contact / Talking

-Move Directly to Car / Lockers

- Post Game Review Off Field

How the Crew Will Handle

-Look Back Violations

- Run Down Plays

- Interference / Obstruction

- Dugout Decorum

- Unruly Spectators

- Bat (and Helmet) Checks

© 2017 – 60 Seconds on Officiating – Created by Billy Martin

111

The Art of the Chase – Crew of 2

Prepared by Billy Martin

Why	**CCP** Move Toward a Credible Calling Position	**ADT** 1st = Angle 2nd = Distance 3rd = Timing	**PCA** The Split The V The Line/Fence
Who	**PCA Umpire** = First Refusal	**Plate Umpire** Move to CCP on All Fly Balls	**Base Umpire** Only Chases if Appropriate
When	**No Brainers** No Runners On Your Line Dead Ball Areas	**Decisions** Troubled Ball Converging Home Run Fence	**Never Go** Routine Can-of-Corn
What	**PPP** PU = Inside / Out BU = Outside / In Think: "IGO / UGO"	**Commit** Verbal Physical	**Mechanics** Go (ADT) Stop / Signal Return When ?

Expanded Pregame Discussion Points

CCP = Credible Calling Position   PCA = Primary Coverage Area
PPP = Pre-Pitch Preparation   PU = Plate Umpire   BU= Base Umpire
Visit "BlueBook60.com" for more information regarding these tools.

Made in the USA
San Bernardino, CA
25 September 2017